ISBN 978-1-334-80638-4
PIBN 10556143

This book is a reproduction of an important historical work. Forgotten Books uses state-of-the-art technology to digitally reconstruct the work, preserving the original format whilst repairing imperfections present in the aged copy. In rare cases, an imperfection in the original, such as a blemish or missing page, may be replicated in our edition. We do, however, repair the vast majority of imperfections successfully; any imperfections that remain are intentionally left to preserve the state of such historical works.

English
Français
Deutsche
Italiano
Español
Português

# www.forgottenbooks.com

**Mythology** Photography **Fiction**
Fishing Christianity **Art** Cooking
Essays Buddhism Freemasonry
Medicine **Biology** Music **Ancient**
**Egypt** Evolution Carpentry Physics
Dance Geology **Mathematics** Fitness
Shakespeare **Folklore** Yoga Marketing
**Confidence** Immortality Biographies
Poetry **Psychology** Witchcraft
Electronics Chemistry History **Law**
Accounting **Philosophy** Anthropology
Alchemy Drama Quantum Mechanics
Atheism Sexual Health **Ancient History**
**Entrepreneurship** Languages Sport
Paleontology Needlework Islam
**Metaphysics** Investment Archaeology
Parenting Statistics Criminology
**Motivational**

# ADMINISTRATION'S FOREST ECOSYSTEM MANAGE-
# MENT PLAN FOR THE PACIFIC NORTHWEST

Y 4. AG 8/1: 103-32

Administration's Forest Ecosystem M...

# HEARING

RE THE

## N SPECIALTY CROPS
## AND NATURAL RESOURCES

OF THE

# COMMITTEE ON AGRICULTURE

AND THE

## SUBCOMMITTEE ON
## NATIONAL PARKS, FORESTS AND PUBLIC LANDS

OF THE

# COMMITTEE ON
# NATURAL RESOURCES

AND THE

## SUBCOMMITTEE ON
## ENVIRONMENT AND NATURAL RESOURCES

OF THE

# COMMITTEE ON
# MERCHANT MARINE AND FISHERIES
# HOUSE OF REPRESENTATIVES

ONE HUNDRED THIRD CONGRESS

FIRST SESSION

AUGUST 3, 1993

**Serial No. 103–32**
(Committee on Agriculture)

**Serial No. 103–45**
(Committee on Natural Resources)

**Serial No. 103–63**
(Committee on Merchant Marine and Fisheries)

Printed for the use of the Committee on Agriculture, Committee on Natural
Resources, and Committee on Merchant Marine and Fisheries

U.S. GOVERNMENT PRINTING OFFICE

75–978                    WASHINGTON : 1994

# ADMINISTRATION'S FOREST ECOSYSTEM MANAGEMENT PLAN FOR THE PACIFIC NORTHWEST

Y 4. AG 8/1: 103-32

Administration's Forest Ecosystem M...

## HEARING

ʙʀᴇ ᴛʜᴇ

N SPECIALTY CROPS
AND NATURAL RESOURCES

ᴏꜰ ᴛʜᴇ

## COMMITTEE ON AGRICULTURE

ᴀɴᴅ ᴛʜᴇ

SUBCOMMITTEE ON
NATIONAL PARKS, FORESTS AND PUBLIC LANDS

ᴏꜰ ᴛʜᴇ

## COMMITTEE ON
## NATURAL RESOURCES

ᴀɴᴅ ᴛʜᴇ

SUBCOMMITTEE ON
ENVIRONMENT AND NATURAL RESOURCES

ᴏꜰ ᴛʜᴇ

## COMMITTEE ON
## MERCHANT MARINE AND FISHERIES
## HOUSE OF REPRESENTATIVES

ONE HUNDRED THIRD CONGRESS

FIRST SESSION

AUGUST 3, 1993

### Serial No. 103-32
(Committee on Agriculture)

### Serial No. 103-45
(Committee on Natural Resources)

### Serial No. 103-63
(Committee on Merchant Marine and Fisheries)

Printed for the use of the Committee on Agriculture, Committee on Natural
Resources, and Committee on Merchant Marine and Fisheries

U.S. GOVERNMENT PRINTING OFFICE

75–978                          WASHINGTON : 1994

# COMMITTEE ON AGRICULTURE

### E (KIKA) DE LA GARZA, Texas, *Chairman*

GEORGE E. BROWN, JR., California,
*Vice Chairman*
CHARLIE ROSE, North Carolina
GLENN ENGLISH, Oklahoma
DAN GLICKMAN, Kansas
CHARLES W. STENHOLM, Texas
HAROLD L. VOLKMER, Missouri
TIMOTHY J. PENNY, Minnesota
TIM JOHNSON, South Dakota
BILL SARPALIUS, Texas
JILL L. LONG, Indiana
GARY A. CONDIT, California
COLLIN C. PETERSON, Minnesota
CALVIN M. DOOLEY, California
EVA M. CLAYTON, North Carolina
DAVID MINGE, Minnesota
EARL F. HILLIARD, Alabama
JAY INSLEE, Washington
THOMAS J. BARLOW III, Kentucky
EARL POMEROY, North Dakota
TIM HOLDEN, Pennsylvania
CYNTHIA A. McKINNEY, Georgia
SCOTTY BAESLER, Kentucky
KAREN L. THURMAN, Florida
SANFORD D. BISHOP, JR., Georgia
BENNIE G. THOMPSON, Mississippi
SAM FARR, California
PAT WILLIAMS, Montana
BLANCHE M. LAMBERT, Arkansas

PAT ROBERTS, Kansas,
*Ranking Minority Member*
BILL EMERSON, Missouri
STEVE GUNDERSON, Wisconsin
TOM LEWIS, Florida
ROBERT F. (BOB) SMITH, Oregon
LARRY COMBEST, Texas
WAYNE ALLARD, Colorado
BILL BARRETT, Nebraska
JIM NUSSLE, Iowa
JOHN A. BOEHNER, Ohio
THOMAS W. EWING, Illinois
JOHN T. DOOLITTLE, California
JACK KINGSTON, Georgia
BOB GOODLATTE, Virginia
JAY DICKEY, Arkansas
RICHARD W. POMBO, California
CHARLES T. CANADY, Florida
NICK SMITH, Michigan
TERRY EVERETT, Alabama

### PROFESSIONAL STAFF

DIANNE POWELL, *Staff Director*
VERNIE HUBERT, *Chief Counsel and Legislative Director*
GARY R. MITCHELL, *Minority Staff Director*
JAMES A. DAVIS, *Press Secretary*

---

## SUBCOMMITTEE ON SPECIALTY CROPS AND NATURAL RESOURCES

### CHARLIE ROSE, North Carolina, *Chairman*

SCOTTY BAESLER, Kentucky,
*Vice Chairman*
SANFORD D. BISHOP, JR., Georgia
GEORGE E. BROWN, JR., California
GARY A. CONDIT, California
EVA M. CLAYTON, North Carolina
KAREN L. THURMAN, Florida
DAVID MINGE, Minnesota
JAY INSLEE, Washington
EARL POMEROY, North Dakota
GLENN ENGLISH, Oklahoma
CHARLES W. STENHOLM, Texas
COLLIN C. PETERSON, Minnesota
SAM FARR, California
HAROLD L. VOLKMER, Missouri

TOM LEWIS, Florida
BILL EMERSON, Missouri
JOHN T. DOOLITTLE, California
JACK KINGSTON, Georgia
BOB GOODLATTE, Virginia
JAY DICKEY, Arkansas
RICHARD W. POMBO, California
TERRY EVERETT, Alabama

(II)

III

## COMMITTEE ON NATURAL RESOURCES

GEORGE MILLER, California, *Chairman*

PHILIP R. SHARP, Indiana
EDWARD J. MARKEY, Massachusetts
AUSTIN J. MURPHY, Pennsylvania
NICK JOE RAHALL II, West Virginia
BRUCE F. VENTO, Minnesota
PAT WILLIAMS, Montana
RON DE LUGO, Virgin Islands
SAM GEJDENSON, Connecticut
RICHARD H. LEHMAN, California
BILL RICHARDSON, New Mexico
PETER A. DeFAZIO, Oregon
ENI F.H. FALEOMAVAEGA, American
 Samoa
TIM JOHNSON, South Dakota
LARRY LaROCCO, Idaho
NEIL ABERCROMBIE, Hawaii
CALVIN M. DOOLEY, California
CARLOS ROMERO-BARCELO, Puerto Rico
KARAN ENGLISH, Arizona
KAREN SHEPHERD, Utah
NATHAN DEAL, Georgia
MAURICE D. HINCHEY, New York
ROBERT A. UNDERWOOD, Guam
SAM FARR, California
LANE EVANS, Illinois
PATSY T. MINK, Hawaii
THOMAS J. BARLOW III, Kentucky
THOMAS M. BARRETT, Wisconsin

DON YOUNG, Alaska,
 *Ranking Republican Member*
JAMES V. HANSEN, Utah
BARBARA F. VUCANOVICH, Nevada
ELTON GALLEGLY, California
ROBERT F. SMITH, Oregon
CRAIG THOMAS, Wyoming
JOHN J. DUNCAN, JR., Tennessee
JOEL HEFLEY, Colorado
JOHN T. DOOLITTLE, California
WAYNE ALLARD, Colorado
RICHARD H. BAKER, Louisiana
KEN CALVERT, California
SCOTT McINNIS, Colorado
RICHARD W. POMBO, California
JAY DICKEY, Arkansas

JOHN LAWRENCE, *Staff Director*
RICHARD MELTZER, *General Counsel*
DANIEL VAL KISH, *Republican Staff Director*

## SUBCOMMITTEE ON NATIONAL PARKS, FORESTS AND PUBLIC LANDS

BRUCE F. VENTO, Minnesota, *Chairman*

EDWARD J. MARKEY, Massachusetts
NICK JOE RAHALL II, West Virginia
PAT WILLIAMS, Montana
PETER A. DeFAZIO, Oregon
TIM JOHNSON, South Dakota
LARRY LaROCCO, Idaho
NEIL ABERCROMBIE, Hawaii
CARLOS ROMERO-BARCELO, Puerto Rico
KARAN ENGLISH, Arizona
KAREN SHEPHERD, Utah
MAURICE D. HINCHEY, New York
ROBERT A. UNDERWOOD, Guam
AUSTIN J. MURPHY, Pennsylvania
BILL RICHARDSON, New Mexico
PATSY T. MINK, Hawaii

JAMES V. HANSEN, Utah,
 *Ranking Republican Member*
ROBERT F. SMITH, Oregon
CRAIG THOMAS, Wyoming
JOHN J. DUNCAN, JR., Tennessee
JOEL HEFLEY, Colorado
JOHN T. DOOLITTLE, California
RICHARD H. BAKER, Louisiana
KEN CALVERT, California
JAY DICKEY, Arkansas

RICHARD HEALY, *Staff Director*
JAMES BRADLEY, *Professional Staff Member*
GWYN FLETCHER, *Staff Assistant*
TED CASE, *Republican Consultant on Oversight & Investigations*

IV

## COMMITTEE ON MERCHANT MARINE AND FISHERIES

GERRY E. STUDDS, Massachusetts, *Chairman*

WILLIAM J. HUGHES, New Jersey
EARL HUTTO, Florida
W.J. (BILLY) TAUZIN, Louisiana
WILLIAM O. LIPINSKI, Illinois
SOLOMON P. ORTIZ, Texas
THOMAS J. MANTON, New York
OWEN B. PICKETT, Virginia
GEORGE J. HOCHBRUECKNER, New York
FRANK PALLONE, JR., New Jersey
GREG LAUGHLIN, Texas
JOLENE UNSOELD, Washington
GENE TAYLOR, Mississippi
JACK REED, Rhode Island
H. MARTIN LANCASTER, North Carolina
THOMAS H. ANDREWS, Maine
ELIZABETH FURSE, Oregon
LYNN SCHENK, California
GENE GREEN, Texas
ALCEE L. HASTINGS, Florida
DAN HAMBURG, California
BLANCHE M. LAMBERT, Arkansas
ANNA G. ESHOO, California
THOMAS J. BARLOW III, Kentucky
BART STUPAK, Michigan
BENNIE G. THOMPSON, Mississippi
MARIA CANTWELL, Washington
PETER DEUTSCH, Florida
GARY L. ACKERMAN, New York

JACK FIELDS, Texas
DON YOUNG, Alaska
HERBERT H. BATEMAN, Virginia
JIM SAXTON, New Jersey
HOWARD COBLE, North Carolina
CURT WELDON, Pennsylvania
JAMES M. INHOFE, Oklahoma
ARTHUR RAVENEL, JR., South Carolina
WAYNE T. GILCHREST, Maryland
RANDY "DUKE" CUNNINGHAM, California
JACK KINGSTON, Georgia
TILLIE K. FOWLER, Florida
MICHAEL N. CASTLE, Delaware
PETER T. KING, New York
LINCOLN DIAZ-BALART, Florida
RICHARD W. POMBO, California
HELEN DELICH BENTLEY, Maryland
CHARLES H. TAYLOR, North Carolina
PETER G. TORKILDSEN, Massachusetts

JEFFERY R. PIKE, *Staff Director*
THOMAS R. KITSOS, *Chief Counsel*
MARY J. FUSCO KITSOS, *Chief Clerk*
HARRY F. BURROUGHS, *Minority Staff Director*

---

### SUBCOMMITTEE ON ENVIRONMENT AND NATURAL RESOURCES

GERRY E. STUDDS, Massachusetts, *Chairman*

GEORGE J. HOCHBRUECKNER, New York
FRANK PALLONE, JR., New Jersey
GREG LAUGHLIN, Texas
JOLENE UNSOELD, Washington
JACK REED, Rhode Island
ELIZABETH FURSE, Oregon
DAN HAMBURG, California
BLANCHE M. LAMBERT, Arkansas
ANNA G. ESHOO, California
EARL HUTTO, Florida
W.J. (BILLY) TAUZIN, Louisiana
SOLOMON P. ORTIZ, Texas
BENNIE G. THOMPSON, Mississippi

JIM SAXTON, New Jersey
DON YOUNG, Alaska
CURT WELDON, Pennsylvania
ARTHUR RAVENEL, JR., South Carolina
WAYNE T. GILCHREST, Maryland
RANDY "DUKE" CUNNINGHAM, California
MICHAEL N. CASTLE, Delaware
CHARLES H. TAYLOR, North Carolina
JACK FIELDS, Texas (Ex Officio)

DANIEL ASHE, *Staff Director*
GINA DEFERRARI, *Professional Staff*
LAUREL BRYANT, *Minority Professional Staff*

# CONTENTS

# ADMINISTRATION'S FOREST ECOSYSTEM MANAGEMENT PLAN FOR THE PACIFIC NORTHWEST

## TUESDAY, AUGUST 3, 1993

HOUSE OF REPRESENTATIVES; SUBCOMMITTEE ON SPE-
CIALTY CROPS AND NATURAL RESOURCES; COMMITTEE
ON AGRICULTURE; JOINT WITH SUBCOMMITTEE ON NA-
TIONAL PARKS, FORESTS AND PUBLIC LANDS; COMMIT-
TEE ON NATURAL RESOURCES; AND SUBCOMMITTEE ON
ENVIRONMENT AND NATURAL RESOURCES; COMMITTEE
ON MERCHANT MARINE AND FISHERIES,

*Washington, DC.*

The subcommittees met, pursuant to call, at 10:15 a.m., in room 1300, Longworth House Office Building, Hon. Charlie Rose (chairman of the Subcommittee on Specialty Crops and Natural Resources) presiding, together with Hon. Bruce. F. Vento (chairman of the Subcommittee on National Parks, Forests and Public Lands); and Hon. Gerry E. Studds (chairman of the Subcommittee on Environment and Natural Resources).

Present from the Subcommittee on Specialty Crops and Natural Resources: Representatives Rose, Baesler, Brown, Condit, Pomeroy, English, Stenholm, Peterson, Farr, Volkmer, Lewis, Doolittle, Kingston, Goodlatte, Pombo, and Everett.

Present from the Subcommittee on National Parks, Forests and Public Lands: Representatives Vento, Williams, DeFazio, LaRocco, Romero-Barceló, Shepherd, Hinchey, Miller, Smith of Oregon, Thomas, and Doolittle.

Present from the Subcommittee on Environment and Natural Resources: Representatives Studds, Pallone, Unsoeld, Reed, Furse, Hamburg, Eshoo, Hutto, and Taylor of North Carolina.

Also present: Representative Herger.

Staff present from the Committee on Agriculture: Andy Baker, assistant counsel; Glenda L. Temple, clerk; Keith Pitts; Alex Buell, James A. Davis, and Stacy Steinitz.

Staff present from the Committee on Natural Resources: Gwyn Fletcher, James Bradley, and Lee Forsgren.

Staff present from the Committee on Merchant Marine and Fisheries: Lesli Gray, Sue Waldron, Gina DeFerrari, Tom Melius, JayneAnne Rex, Willie Stelle, and Margherita Woods.

## OPENING STATEMENT OF HON. CHARLIE ROSE, A REPRESENTATIVE IN CONGRESS FROM THE STATE OF NORTH CAROLINA

Mr. ROSE. The subcommittees will come to order.

This is a meeting of the Specialty Crops and Natural Resources Subcommittee of the Committee on Agriculture; the National Parks, Forests and Public Lands Subcommittee of the Committee on Natural Resources; and the Environment and Natural Resources Subcommittee of the Committee on Merchant Marine and Fisheries; a joint public hearing to review the administration's Pacific Northwest forest proposal.

Ladies and gentlemen, I welcome you all to the Agriculture Committee, but I would like to note that we have a rather ambitious schedule today. I would propose that we not make opening statements, but that when you are given an opportunity, as you will be, to question any of the people who have spoken, that you make any such remarks at that time. Also, any prepared statements submitted by the members will appear at this point in the record.

[The prepared statements of Mr. Brown, Mr. Condit, Mr. Herger, and Mrs. Unsoeld follow:]

# REMARKS

# PREPARED FOR PRESENTATION

# BY CONGRESSMAN GEORGE E. BROWN, JR.

# AT JOINT SUBCOMMITTEE HEARINGS

# IN THE U. S. HOUSE OF REPRESENTATIVES

# ON THE CLINTON ADMINISTRATION'S PLAN

# ON NORTHWEST FORESTS

# 3 AUGUST 1993

THANK YOU, MR. CHAIRMAN....

MR. SECRETARY -- JIM -- IT'S VERY GOOD TO HAVE YOU, MR. COLLINS FROM THE INTERIOR DEPARTMENT, THESE DISTINGUISHED SCIENTISTS, AND YOUR OTHER COLLEAGUES HERE TODAY, AND I WANT TO WELCOME YOU. AND TO YOU JIM, I WANT TO SAY WELCOME BACK.

THE PRESIDENT SAID THAT HIS ADMINISTRATION'S PLAN ON THE NORTHWEST FORESTS WOULD NOT PLEASE EVERYBODY -- THAT'S FOR SURE -- BUT HE ALSO SAID THAT IT PROBABLY WOULD NOT PLEASE ANYBODY. WELL, I HATE TO CONTRADICT THE PRESIDENT, BUT I FEEL HE WAS WRONG. IN FACT, THE PLAN THAT YOU ARE HERE TO

DISCUSS TODAY PLEASES ME. IT PLEASES ME VERY MUCH. THAT IS NOT TO SAY THAT I DON'T HAVE QUESTIONS ABOUT CERTAIN ASPECTS OF THE PLAN. YOU WILL HAVE A CHANCE TO RESPOND TO MY QUESTIONS LATER. THE PLAN CERTAINLY IS NOT EVERYTHING THAT I WOULD LIKE TO HAVE SEEN IN A PERFECT WORLD. BUT I WANT TO SAY UP FRONT THAT THE PLAN THAT YOU HAVE COME UP WITH IS A VERY GOOD PLAN.

I AM IMPRESSED WITH THE EFFORT THAT YOU AND MANY OTHERS HAVE EXPENDED IN THE FORMULATION OF THIS PLAN. THIS WAS NO EASY TASK. AND I THINK THAT YOU ARE TO CONGRATULATED.

I AM ESPECIALLY IMPRESSED WITH THE

SCIENTIFIC INPUT IN TERMS OF YOUR DECISION-

MAKING. THE QUESTION OF SCIENCE AND ITS

APPLICATION TO THE ISSUES FACING OUR SOCIETY IS

OF COURSE VERY NEAR AND DEAR TO ME. A

SCIENTIFIC BASIS FOR DECISION-MAKING ON THESE

CONTENTIOUS ISSUES WAS ONE OF THE CRITERIA

THAT I AND MANY OF MY COLLEAGUES -- NOTABLY

MY GOOD FRIEND CHAIRMAN VENTO -- INDICATED

WAS NECESSARY TO WIN OUR SUPPORT AND, I

BELIEVE, TO SERVE THE INTEREST OF ALL THE

PEOPLE OF THIS GREAT COUNTRY. I WANT TO THANK

YOU FOR YOUR HARD WORK, AND I WANT TO THANK

YOUR FINE SCIENTIFIC TEAM, ESPECIALLY DR.

THOMAS, FOR THEIR REMARKABLE EFFORT. YOU

HAVE DONE A FINE JOB. THIS IS A VERY

SCIENTIFICALLY CREDIBLE DOCUMENT.

CERTAIN ASPECTS OF THE PLAN NEED REFINING AND REALIGNING IN MY OPINION. I HOPE THAT WE CAN BEGIN A DIALOGUE ON THESE ISSUES TODAY. AND, MR. SECRETARY, I HOPE YOU WILL BE WILLING TO ANSWER FURTHER QUESTIONS IN WRITING. *(PAUSE FOR REPLY.)* HOWEVER, I AM GLAD TO INDICATE THAT YOU HAVE MY SUPPORT. AND I WILL DO WHAT I CAN TO SEE THAT THIS PLAN IS IMPLEMENTED. ...THANK YOU VERY MUCH.

DEPARTMENT OF AGRICULTURE
OFFICE OF THE SECRETARY
WASHINGTON, D.C. 20250

September 13, 1993

Honorable Charlie Rose
Chairman, Subcommittee on Special Crops
  and Natural Resources
U.S. House of Representatives
105 Cannon House Office Building
Washington, D.C.  20515-3307

Dear Congressman Rose:

As requested in your letter of August 9, enclosed are the questions and answers relating to my testimony at the August 3 hearing on the Northwest Forest Plan.

If you need further information, please do not hesitate to call me at 720-7173.

Sincerely,

James R. Lyons
Assistant Secretary
Natural Resources and Environment

Enclosure

JRL:jls

Questions and Answers for Congressman George Brown

1. How can you begin to assure me and the American people that this plan will be implemented? What can you tell me that will convince me that the provisions of this plan will be implemented and that I and others can trust the Forest Service to follow the plan as given?

The Administration is committed to moving forward in implementing the Plan. We have established an Interagency Implementation Team composed of Forest Service, Bureau of Land Management, U.S. Fish and Wildlife Service, National Marine Fisheries Service, and Environmental Protection Agency personnel. This team is developing a detailed action plan for implementing the Administration's Forest Plan. In addition, the Regional Interagency Executive Team composed of the regional directors of the previously mentioned agencies met last week to discuss the steps each agency is taking to implement the Plan.

You have my personal assurance that all of the agencies are committed to implementing the Plan. In fact, I have personally witnessed enthusiasm by all of the agencies to move forward with the Plan. The successful implementation of the President's Forest Plan will require the support of both the executive and legislative branches. We look forward to working with Congress through the appropriations process to develop a coordinated approach which will ensure the success of the Forest Plan to provide for sound ecological management and end this period of uncertainty for the Pacific Northwest.

2. Can you tell me what snags are?

As defined in the Draft Supplemental Environmental Impact Statement for managing habitat within the range of the northern spotted owl and FEMAT, snags are ". . . any standing dead, partially dead, or defective (cull) tree at least 10 inches in diameter at breast height and at least six feet tall."

3. What kind of trees do owls and other raptors like to nest in?

There are three federally-listed raptor species within the range of the northern spotted owl. The northern spotted owl typically nests in cavities or on platforms of conifer trees. Bald eagles tend to use large, old trees near water. Peregrine falcons nest on cliff ledges.

4. How is it that this plan calls for salvage and thinning timber harvest in the proposed reserves? What kind of trees do you plan to salvage?.....etc.

Under the preferred alternative, salvage, thinning, and other silvicultural treatments would be allowed within late-successional reserves only if they are neutral or beneficial to the creation and maintenance of late-successional forest conditions. All silvicultural treatments would be reviewed by an interagency oversight team to ensure they are neutral or beneficial. All salvage of dead trees would be limited to areas where catastrophic loss exceeded 10 acres. Thinning of green trees would be limited only to young stands 80 years or less in age. Salvage would be based on guidelines adapted from the Final Draft Recovery Plan for the Northern Spotted Owl developed by the USDI Recovery Team.

5. Why can't you just leave these areas alone?

Salvage of dead trees from areas affected by extensive catastrophic loss or thinning of dense young stands are ecologically sound management options. The goal of late-successional reserves is to foster late-successional forest conditions. In extensive areas of dead trees, the likelihood of additional stand-replacing events, such as fire, is greater than in a healthy forest. Natural regeneration of these areas may be reduced by the existence of heavy woody debris. If another stand-replacing event occurs or natural regeneration is slowed, it will take longer for late-successional forest conditions to be attained. Similarly, the development of such conditions can be advanced by careful thinning of dense young stands. Thus, salvage of dead trees from extensively impacted areas and thinning of young stands, under the supervision of an oversight team, could help Federal agencies meet the goals of the late-successional reserves.

6. Don't dead trees, both standing and fallen, provide significant habitat for a variety of wildlife and essential forest microorganisms?

Dead trees do, indeed, provide significant habitat for a wide variety of wildlife species and forest microorganisms. It is the intent of the late-successional reserves to only remove these dead trees when their continued existence in the reserve could hinder the attainment of late-successional forest conditions. It should also be noted that even outside of the reserves, in the matrix, there are guidelines for the retention of both green trees and snags to benefit wildlife species and the forest ecosystem.

*Statement*
*by*
*Congressman Gary A. Condit*

**Subcommittee on Specialty Crops & Natural Resources**

*Joint public hearing with*

**Subcommittee on National Parks, Forests, and Public Lands
and the Subcommittee on Environment and Natural Resources**

**Regarding Review of Administration's Pacific Northwest Forest
Proposal (Option 9)**

**August 2, 1993**

During the past three years, thousands of my constituents have communicated their concerns regarding national forest issues and the U.S. Forest Service. While many issues have been raised and many opinions expressed, the most frequently voiced concern from my district has been the preservation for future generations of the last remaining remnant of old growth ancient forest in the Pacific Northwest. I have been and continue to be supportive of the interest shown by my constituents in this matter, and accordingly I welcome the early initiatives of President Clinton and Vice-President Gore to work towards a permanent resolution of the forest issue that is both scientifically sound and economically wise.

I have suggested that any forest plan should focus primarily on good science and sound economics, rather than on the politics of the issue. The essential need is to couple the permanent protection gained from statutory designation of ancient forest reserves with strong economic measures to benefit rural communities and timber workers. We must cope with both ecological and economic threats, during the coming transition to a sustainable timber economy and to economically diversified rural communities. The Administration's "Option 9" forest plan is an attempt to resolve the controversy over forest management in the Pacific Northwest. Because of the longstanding polarization of interests, it is virtually impossible to craft a plan that would be widely accepted and it is my hope that all parties involved can move towards a resolution. Please be assured that I plan to work with Members of Congress and the Administration for a plan that is reasonable and fair.

(Attachment follows:)

13

# Building Industry Association
## of
## Central California, Inc.

1401 "F" STREET

BIACC

PHONE 529-4531                                    MODESTO, CA 95354

July 7, 1993

The Honorable Gary Condit
U.S. House of Representatives
Washington, DC  20515

Dear Representative Condit:

As an executive officer of a builders association, I am writing to
express my severe disappointment with the President's recently
released Forest Plan.  While he has tried to paint the timber
crisis as a regional problem, he cannot ignore the fact that it is
truly a national issue.  The impact this plan could have on home
building can deal a serious blow to economic recovery, not just in
the Northwest, but nationwide.  Indeed, the President pledged to
not forget the human and economic dimensions of the timber crisis,
but it appears as though that is exactly what he has done.

I am extremely concerned about what the level of harvest called for
in this plan will do to lumber prices.  As you recall, due to
concern over the lack of supply in March, prices rose to an all-
time high of $507 per 1000 board feet.  At that level, $5,000 is
added to the cost of an average home, and 130,000 potential home
buyers are priced out of the market.  The result is thousands of
jobs being lost in the construction industry.  The President's plan
could well cause prices to go even higher -- and he knows it.  If
this isn't forgetting humans and the economy, I don't know what is.

The only hope left for the home buyers and workers of this country
is for Congress to develop a plan of its own.  I have been pleased
to hear of Speaker Foley's adamant opposition to the Forest Plan
and his call for a revision of the Endangered Species Act (ESA).  I
hope that you will urge the Speaker to take the lead in both
revising the ESA and in developing a reasonable, rational
legislative solution to the timber crisis.

Homes are built in every town in every state of the Union, and in
every town in every state of the Union the effect of this plan will
be felt.  I urge you to take action as soon as possible.

Sincerely,

Edward P. Taczanowsky
Executive Vice President

EPT:mb

STATEMENT OF THE HONORABLE WALLY HERGER

HOUSE AGRICULTURE COMMITTEE

SUBCOMMITTEE ON SPECIALTY CROPS AND NATURAL RESOURCES

AUGUST 3, 1993

Mr. Chairman, I want to commend you for holding this hearing to review President Clinton's Forestry Proposal. I also greatly appreciate your willingness to allow me to sit with this Subcommittee for this important hearing.

At the Portland Forest Conference, President Clinton pledged to find a "balanced" solution to the crisis that is gripping the timber-dependent communities of northern California, Oregon and Washington. However, despite the fact that roughly 70 to 80 percent of our forests in California are already off limits to timber harvesting, "Option 9" calls for a 70% reduction in timber harvests from historical levels. This will ensure that thousands of jobs will be lost in the coming months in communities that already have unemployment levels more than double the national average. For example, Trinity County, a timber-dependent county in my district, has an unemployment rate of 15.4. Also, the reduction in harvests from federal lands will certainly drive up lumber prices in the future, and this ultimately will further hinder economic growth throughout the nation. As such, the President's plan fails to provide the needed balance from either a regional or national perspective.

Option 9 also fails to address the unique biological characteristics of the forests in northern California. The most

recent science clearly indicates that drastic reductions in
timber harvests are not necessary in order to protect spotted
owls or old growth forests. We have documented at least four
times more spotted owls than the Fish and Wildlife Service
estimated existed when it listed the species under the Endangered
Species Act. In fact, the California Forestry Association has
announced that it is in the process of formally petitioning for
the de-listing of the owl in California.

Finally, our forests in California have historically been
more vulnerable to catastrophic wildfires, and need to be managed
for both fire prevention and the maintenance of forest health.
Option 9, by severely limiting management activities through the
implementation of a reserve system, will significantly impede
these objectives, thus putting human lives and the health of
forests in danger.

The people of northern California are deeply disappointed
that the President's plan is not balanced and does not address
the unique characteristics of California's forests. They are not
willing to accept temporary government make-work jobs in exchange
for permanent family-wage jobs provided by the timber industry.
The Administration should immediately convene a panel of
scientists whose objective is to specifically review the
management of California's forests. The California Forestry
Association has recently developed an eco-system management
approach which should be reviewed by such a panel. In the
interim, Congress should move immediately to pass legislation
which allows sufficient timber harvest to sustain our communities

and provide for healthy forests.

I look forward to hearing the Administration's testimony, and again would like to thank the Chairman for this opportunity to express my concerns.

**Statement by the Honorable Jolene Unsoeld (D-WA)**
**On the President's Forest Plan**
**Joint Agriculture, Natural Resources and Merchant**
**Marine and Fisheries Subcommittee Hearing**
**August 3, 1993**

I want to thank Chairmen Studds, Vento and Rose for conducting this hearing on the President's Northwest forest proposal.

This hearing, like the President's plan, looks to the future and moves us beyond the gridlock of the past. It is about moving beyond the mismanagement that undermined both healthy forest ecosystems and timber-dependent communities, that decimated our watersheds and tore into shreds our resource-based economy.

Given the years of mismanagement, the dependence of local economies on our forest resources, and the pain and suffering of the families in our timber communities, it's no surprise that many are critical of the Administration proposal. But as we hear more about the plan today, let's focus our discussion on the merits of the initiative and on the need to move into a new era of resource stewardship.

This new era means a shift from the narrow, short-term, profit-based resource management policies that led us into a species-by-species crisis to a broader ecosystem management approach that addresses habitat and human needs. We must understand -- as the Administration plan does -- that watershed protection and ecosystem health hold the key to sustainable use of our resources. They hold the key to rejecting the status quo of paralysis, of frustrating failures to reach a consensus, and of rhetorical debates that produced plenty of false hopes but precious few solutions.

I look forward to hearing from the witnesses before us today and again want to thank our Chairmen for their efforts.

Mr. ROSE. Is there any serious objection to that? If not, I would welcome Mr. Tom Collier, the Chief of Staff, U.S. Department of the Interior, Washington, DC.

All right, we will go ahead, Mr. Collier. We are happy to hear from you.

## STATEMENT OF TOM COLLIER, CHIEF OF STAFF, U.S. DEPARTMENT OF THE INTERIOR, ACCOMPANIED BY JACK WARD THOMAS, CHIEF, RESEARCH WILDLIFE BIOLOGIST, U.S. FOREST SERVICE, PACIFIC NORTHWEST RESEARCH STATION, LA GRANDE, OR; JAMES R. SEDELL, PRINCIPAL RESEARCH ECOLOGIST, U.S. FOREST SERVICE, PACIFIC NORTHWEST RESEARCH STATION, CORVALLIS, OR; K. NORMAN JOHNSON, PROFESSOR, DEPARTMENT OF FOREST RESOURCES, OREGON STATE UNIVERSITY; BRIAN GREBER, ASSOCIATE PROFESSOR, FOREST RESOURCES ECONOMICS, COLLEGE OF FORESTRY, OREGON STATE UNIVERSITY; ROGER N. CLARK, PROGRAM MANAGER, FOREST RESOURCES ECONOMICS, COLLEGE OF FORESTRY, OREGON STATE UNIVERSITY; AND JERRY F. FRANKLIN, PROFESSOR, ECOSYSTEM ANALYSIS, COLLEGE OF FOREST RESOURCES, UNIVERSITY OF WASHINGTON

Mr. COLLIER. Thank you. Good morning, Mr. Chairman, and members of the subcommittees. I ask permission to submit my full testimony for the record.

Mr. ROSE. Without objection.

Mr. COLLIER. Thank you, sir.

I would like to talk briefly about the basic elements of the President's package; also about how we intend to implement it, but most of all, I would like to spend a few minutes talking about how we got where we are today.

I think that the context of these issues is extremely important, primarily because it defines the very narrow decisional space that I believe the President has or had when he addressed this issue; and second, I think it shows what a clean break this administration is breaking from the past.

The history of forest management in this region has been one of both shortsightedness and deliberate procrastination. The Government knew for a long time that it was cutting too much timber and there were countless warnings, but it ignored those warnings. The Government also knew that the laws that controlled the cutting of that timber were not complex, not too difficult to deal with, and yet it ignored those laws and blamed it on that complexity.

Our Government, in my opinion, set out deliberately to become boxed in and it did so so that it could try to gut the environmental laws that are controlling.

Well, I think the Government succeeded in being boxed in. Everything in the Northwest was brought to a complete standstill, but I don't think it succeeded in gutting the environmental laws, because the plan that we are bringing forth is one that complies with those laws.

What they did, though, when they created that box was to steal much of the decisional space that we had when we looked at this issue. An earlier plan, a responsible plan, would have been a much better one. It would not have caused, I think, the damage that this one will cause to a number of the communities in the Northwest.

I think many of you have often read or heard Secretary Babbitt speak of how it is his intention to show how the environmental statutes in this country can be managed in a way to avoid train wrecks. But in the Northwest, we are not avoiding a train wreck, what we are doing there is cleaning up after one and there have been a number of victims: The timber workers, mills, families that have been affected by this.

All of that occurred, I believe, because the many warnings that were sounded were ignored. There were numerous scientific warnings. These were not just the warnings of one rogue scientist in the Northwest, and not just the warnings of the so-called "Gang of Four," but there were a number of scientists from 1980 forward who said, you are cutting too much timber, and Government ignored those warnings.

There were a number of legal warnings also, and I think everyone has heard of Judge Dwyer and his opinions in the Northwest. But in addition to Judge Dwyer, enough judges have looked at this issue to field an entire baseball team, and every one of those nine, plus Judge Dwyer, have concluded that Federal timber management policies were not in compliance with the law.

I think that some folks have blamed those judicial decisions on the fact that the laws were hypertechnical or that there had been hypertechnical violations of the statutes, but that is not the case. The violations of the laws that led to the injunction in the Northwest were gross violations of the law. They were easy decisions for those judges to make.

I have also heard that the judges that made these decisions were predisposed to rule in favor of the environmental community. Well, let me tell you that most of those judges were appointed by the same administration whose decisions they were in fact reviewing.

Now, one example of the kind of facts that led to one of these decisions. In 1987, the Bureau of Land Management came up with a new plan to manage its forests in the Northwest, but it announced that it was going to rely on an environmental impact statement for that plan that had been drafted prior to 1983, 4 years.

And in those intervening 4 years, five significant facts had occurred: The Fish and Wildlife Service had done a new status review; the Forest Service had drafted a supplemental EIS; a blue ribbon panel of scientists had completed an owl study; a leading scientist had published a population demographics and viability review; and BLM's own biologists had done a new owl report. None of that was considered by BLM. The obvious result was that Judge Helen Frye ruled that BLM was in violation of NEPA.

On review of this order, the appellate court stated that this was a deliberate protracted refusal to comply with applicable environmental laws. It is the same kind of facts that led Judge Dwyer at one point to say the following:

"More is involved here than a simple failure by an agency to comply with its governing statute. The most recent violation of NFMA exemplifies a deliberate and systematic refusal by the Forest Service and the Fish and Wildlife Service to comply with the laws protecting wildlife. This is not the doing of the scientists, the foresters, rangers, and others at the working levels of these agencies. It reflects decisions made by higher authorities in the executive branch of government."

When you read through all these cases that stack about so high, it makes you angry. There is an unmistakable attempt demonstrated by the facts in those cases to frustrate the will of Congress, to frustrate the will of these committees, and the consequences to the members of the communities in the Northwest have been extraordinary.

It is not my intent today to point blame or to assess blame. The point I am trying to make, though, is that when we were faced with this issue, we were not writing on a clean slate. As a result of the deliberate systematic refusals, in Judge Dwyer's words, to follow the law, there were no timber sales that could be made from Federal lands in the Northwest. The process was shut down when we walked in. The pipeline was running dry.

The issue that we faced was not whether we should try to return to historic cut levels, but the issue was whether we could get any timber out of that region at all, given those injunctions, whether w could break that logjam and whether we could do it immediately.

As I said before, we had a very narrow range of options, but even we did not expect that the numbers that would come out of our plan would be as low as they were. We still think, though, that it is the best plan that is possible. And the reason for the instructions the President gave to the group that put that plan together, first, was that you should comply with the law, and the second is that you should rely on the best science available.

As we struggled through that, we came up with a plan that has some elements that I think clearly make it the best plan available. First, it is an ecosystemwide watershed focused plan. I think, for the first time, we are looking at that entire region and we are looking at those critical watersheds.

Second, it is a plan that complies with the law, but in doing so, it is the plan that complies with the law and maximizes the amount of timber cut that the law will allow.

Third, it avoids a drastic reassessment in the future if new species are listed under the Endangered Species Act. The fact, we looked at all of the species in the Northwest, at this point, in making our plans, keeps us from having to do that at that type of significant readjustment in the future.

Fourth, I am confident we will withstand court challenges. We have looked to the best science, we have relied on the best science. We have complied with the procedures that the statutes require.

And, finally, we will have a sustainable, reliable level of timber available to those communities into the future. Our challenge now is implementing the plan, and we are only a few weeks into that effort, but we are making some headway. We have a lot of Federal agencies out there that are not used to working together and we are making them work together, and I think we are doing a very good job of that.

In particular, the Agriculture Department under Secretary Espy and the Forest Service under Jim Lyons have been splendid partners as we have worked through this. Jim will talk a little more about the details of the implementation in his testimony.

We recognize that this implementation challenge is going to be a difficult one, but we take very seriously the commitments we have made to the people of the Pacific Northwest and those of us that have looked the President in the eyes and made the same commitment to him take that seriously also.

We are going to bring to bear the resources necessary to implement this plan and to do so as soon as possible.

Thank you, Mr. Chairman.

[The prepared statement of Mr. Collier appears at the conclusion of the hearing.]

Mr. ROSE. Thank you very much.

The Honorable James R. Lyons, Assistant Secretary for Natural Resources and Environment, USDA.

Welcome.

## STATEMENT OF JAMES R. LYONS, ASSISTANT SECRETARY, NATURAL RESOURCES AND ENVIRONMENT, U.S. DEPARTMENT OF AGRICULTURE

Mr. LYONS. Thank you, Mr. Chairman, it is a pleasure to be back home.

I am pleased to join my colleague, Mr. Tom Collier, in appearing before you today to discuss the President's Forest Ecosystem Management Plan for the Pacific Northwest. And I am also pleased to be joined by key members of the Forest Ecosystem Management Assessment Team who will be addressing questions later. In particular, Dr. Jack Ward Thomas who served as the team leader; Dr. James Sedell, who cochaired the aquatic and watershed working group; Dr. K. Norman Johnson, who led the FEMAT team; Dr. Brian Greber, the leader of the economic assessment group; and Dr. Roger Clark, who led the social assessment group.

At the conclusion of the forest conference in Portland, Oregon, President Clinton outlined five principles to guide the crafting of a solution to the forest management conundrum which faces the Pacific Northwest in northern California.

The President stated: "First, we must never forget the human and economic dimensions of these problems. Where sound management policies can preserve the health of forest plans, sales should go forward. Where this requirement cannot be met, we need to do our best to offer new economic opportunities for year-round, high wage, high-skill jobs.

"Second, as we craft the plan, we need to protect the long-term health of our forests, our wildlife, and our waterways. They are a gift from God and we hold them in trust for future generations.

"Third, our efforts must be, insofar as we are wise enough to know it, scientifically sound, ecologically credible, and legally responsible.

"Fourth, the plan should produce a predictable and sustainable level of timber sales and nontimber resources that will not degrade or destroy the environment.

"Fifth, to achieve these goals, we will do our best * * * to make the Federal Government work together and work for you. We may make mistakes, but we will try to end the gridlock within the Federal Government, and we will insist on collaboration, not confrontation."

The President established several working groups to develop options and approaches for achieving these objectives, and my remarks today will focus on the activities of the Forest Ecosystem Management Assessment Team, or FEMAT, as we call it. As my colleague, Mr. Collier, indicated, this issue is strewn with the wreckage of failed attempts to devise and implement a management strategy that is legally sound and/or politically acceptable.

Many of the members of this dais, including two of the three subcommittee chairman here, and Chairman Miller, have invested much time and energy in seeking a resolution to this issue. In fact, the most promising congressional effort to date was the product of the collaborative efforts of the chairmen of the three House committees and the subcommittees who have convened this hearing today.

That collaborative effort generated H.R. 4899, a measure that successfully passed the Committee on Agriculture last Congress only to stall later in the legislative process. That bill, in fact, had elements in common with the President's forest plan.

First, both the resource management strategy embodied in H.R. 4899 and the President's plan are based on a scientifically sound ecosystem oriented set of forest management principles. In short, the strategy embodied in H.R. 4899 and the President's plan sought to move from the species-by-species protection approach of the past to a more integrated multispecies management framework, one that would, as one of your former colleagues, Sid Morrison, stated, diminish the likelihood of the "endangered species of the month" problem.

The second is the management options that would serve as the basis for H.R. 4899 and those which underlie the President's plan were devised by a team of individuals with expertise in forest ecosystems, wildlife management, fisheries biology, hydrology, silviculture, and forest economics. This multidisciplinary approach is essential to understanding the biological, social, and economic ramifications of the strategies selected.

Third, in both instances, the options ranged from those that provide high levels of timber production and, concurrently, lesser protection for old-growth ecosystems and associated animal and plant species to those which protected most, if not all, remaining old growth but, of course, yielded much less timber. Thus, both the President and the congressional authors of H.R. 4899 had a wide range of scientifically based options from which to choose.

Finally, as in the "Gang of Four" exercise which led to development of H.R. 4899, the FEMAT generated options for the President's consideration, but did not choose an alternative. That decision most appropriately was left to policymakers.

The charge given FEMAT by the President was clearly articulated in a letter of instruction to the team. Specifically, FEMAT was instructed to identify and describe management alternatives that attain the greatest economic and social contribution from the forests of the region while meeting the requirements of applicable laws and regulations, including the Endangered Species Act, the

National Forest Management Act, the Federal Land Policy Management Act, and NEPA.

The FEMAT's work benefited from a substantial body of information and analysis stemming from previous efforts to address the various management issues affecting the region.

Specifically, the team benefited from the report of the Interagency Spotted Owl Committee and the draft report of the recovery team for the northern spotted owl. Two reports, by the way, which were developed under guidance of the Bush administration.

In addition, the FEMAT used information generated by the scientific analysis team which developed a strategy for protecting other 1,400 old-growth associated plant and animal species and the PACFISH report which developed a strategy for conservation and management of anadromous fisheries resources in the region.

Finally, the FEMAT also consulted and used the work of the so-called "Gang of Four" which, under the direction of the House Agriculture Committee and the Merchant Marine and Fisheries Committee, identified alternatives for management of late-successional, old-growth forest ecosystems in the Pacific Northwest and northern California.

With these technical studies as a foundation, the FEMAT expanded the scope of its analysis, further refining the more than 40 management options reflected in these prior reports, and identifying yet another set of alternatives.

In total, the FEMAT evaluated a range of 58 options for management of late-successional and old-growth forest in Oregon, Washington, and northern California to determine how the viability of key species of plants and animals might be affected. In all, the viability of over 1,400 plant and animal species was evaluated either individually or by groups.

Option nine—the basis for the President's forest plan—represents a new approach to forest ecosystem management in which watershed management and the protection of riparian areas are critical elements for sustaining forest management in the region. While prior strategies such as the ISC report and the recovery plan for the northern spotted owl were designed to protect owls, the scientific team recognized that attention to watersheds, both for their importance to water quality and critical fisheries, is key to effective multiple-resource management in the region.

Watersheds are the foundation for the conservation strategy embodied in option nine. More efficient use of late-successional reserves could be achieved if they were designed in conjunction with key watersheds and modified to meet other objectives, such as protecting spotted owls.

Option nine provides greater flexibility for management of lands in the late-successional reserve, thinning of young forest stands—up to 80 years of age—by means of enhancing and accelerating the old-growth forest characteristics. In addition, salvage of timber is permitted in such reserves, provided the timbering has a neutral or positive effect on the management objectives of the reserve.

Key watersheds were also designated this option nine to guide future management activities to ensure that sensitive fish stocks and critical water quality areas are not harmed. In addition, a unique aspect of option 9 is the creation of 10 adaptive management areas. These units, ranging in size from 80,000 to 480,000 acres, are intended to promote the development and testing of innovative management strategies to achieve conservation goals and encourage greater public participation in deciding how these forests might be managed.

Much has been made of the anticipated annual timber sale quantities that would result from implementation of option nine. I believe some clarification is warranted.

First, recognize that even current levels of timber harvest from the region are not sustainable if the Forest Service and the Bureau of Land Management are to comply with existing requirements for multiple-use, sustained-yield management in the region.

It is important to recognize a number of factors that have led to what have proven to be overly optimistic projections of allowable sales quantities in the past. The projected annual sale quantity estimates conducted under this analysis sought to correct this problem. In fact, rather than report an estimated annual sale quantity, or ASQ, the FEMAT provides an estimate of PSQ, or probable sale quantity.

PSQ's are intended to reflect realistic expectations of what can be harvested given real world circumstances. Further, management analysis or unit analysis will need to be conducted to verify sustainable harvest levels. However, the PSQ's are an honest attempt to reduce confusion between past projections and current estimates of what can actually be harvested on an annual sustained-yield basis.

The President's forest management plan for the region was presented to Judge William Dwyer on July 16 as the preferred alternative in the draft supplemental EIS for the regional guide for management of the northern spotted owl. In addition, last week the document was issued for public review and comment.

This is the beginning of a process. The final plan will not be in place, should the current schedule be followed, until the end of 1993. However, despite this, the administration is moving forward to use the strategy in its present form to guide future management activities. Should changes in the document occur as a result of public comment, further adjustments will be made accordingly.

A key to implementation is coordination and cooperation among the affected Federal agencies. Last week, a regional interagency coordination team was established in Portland to facilitate development of management activities in the short term in conjunction with the President's plan and to begin the process of establishing the mechanisms for more efficient and effective resource management in the region in the future.

As a part of this effort, a review of all existing enjoined timber sales is being conducted to determine what modifications, if any, may be needed to expedite the preparation and sale. In addition, communications are occurring with the plaintiffs in the Seattle Audubon case to see if we can approach the court to seek some injunctive relief.

In summary, Mr. Chairman, I would like to make the case for why this forest management strategy, the President's forest plan, is the right thing to do. First and foremost, the people of the region and the communities need this issue resolved. The President has put forward a bold, innovative, and, yes, controversial plan to attempt to bring this issue to closure.

But let us not delude ourselves. If this issue had been easier to resolve, you and I and the Bush administration would have done so. This President is willing to make the tough choices and provide the leadership needed to successfully break the logjam that currently exists.

Second, this plan is balanced. I know that our critics look at the 1.2 billion board foot annual sale quantity, compare it to the harvest of the mid-1980's and say, "This is balance?" I must admit Mr. Chairmen, having worked with many of you over the past several years, those numbers are indeed shocking in comparison to the harvest levels of the past decade. However, we realize now that we were cutting timber faster than we could sustain.

This plan is balanced because it seeks to maintain a sustainable Federal timber harvest level without compromising the other natural resources we are entrusted to manage. In addition, we believe that the President's forest plan can provide the basis for substantive relief from the current constraints on private forest lands in the region.

The plan does not protect all remaining old growth. If we are to have a timber supply at all in the region for the foreseeable future, some of it will in fact have to be cut. The plan protects the old growth needed to secure the future of owls, murrelets, fish, and the old-growth ecosystem, while providing a sustainable timber harvest to provide for the security of the communities. This is a rational way to proceed. In fact, I would argue it is the only way to proceed in a legally responsible and rational way.

Finally, Mr. Chairman, this plan is sound and credible because it is firmly based on our knowledge of forestry and in forest ecosystems, and the way in which forestry affects the resources we are entrusted to manage. Some people have criticized the science and the scientists who are part of FEMAT.

These critics argue, "This is not science." Well, you know, they are right. The FEMAT report is not science in the traditional sense. It is the product of the collective expertise of the best scientists and technical experts we could assemble attempting to construct a regional management plan the likes of which has never been created before. In fact, I would argue this is the first real attempt at ecosystem management of the Federal lands we have ever made.

I don't believe we want scientists making the kinds of policy calls that were made in selecting option nine. That is the role of the President and the Congress and people like you and me. I believe, Mr. Chairman, that we have done our job in providing the President with the best information available, and he has done his job and fulfilled his commitment to develop a plan that has logjammed the entire region.

I want to thank you for the opportunity to offer my views and would be glad to respond to any questions you might have.

[The prepared statement of Mr. Lyons appears at the conclusion of the hearing.]

Mr. ROSE. Thank you very much. Before we do that, can we ask Dr. K. Norman Johnson, professor of the department of forest resources, Oregon State University, to give us his presentation and then we will let all of the——

Mr. JOHNSON. Mr. Chairman, I am K. Norman Johnson and I wanted to submit my comments for the record but don't feel the need to read them, but simply respond to questions, if that is OK.

[The prepared statement of Mr. Johnson appears at the conclusion of the hearing.]

Mr. ROSE. All right, that is fine. Would all of the people who are accompanying our two speakers please come around so they can help or at least be on the first row if not sitting at the table. If there is a seat at the table, please sit there.

I only have two questions for Secretary Lyons and Mr. Collier. The forest plan, as I understand it, is a substantial departure from the current policies of the Forest Service. Do you currently have the people, the agency infrastructure, and the funding in place to effectively implement this new policy?

And if not, what help does the administration need from Congress to ensure the success of this new policy?

Mr. Lyons.

Mr. LYONS. Mr. Chairman, we are currently attempting to determine precisely the resources we need to implement the plan. One of the things I did last week in meeting with the senior agency team was to request that they conduct a complete assessment of the resources necessary for implementation.

The President did present the plan to the Congress and has made requests for funding to provide some assistance for implementation. If we obtain that funding, which we hope we will through the Interior Appropriations process, we will proceed with activities such as the watershed restoration work that is called for in the plan.

If we are unable to obtain that money through appropriations, we will seek other means, perhaps through shifting resources around in our existing budget to begin the implementation process.

Mr. ROSE. All right. Mr. Collier.

Mr. COLLIER. Mr. Chairman, we have the same answer.

Mr. ROSE. All right. Last Friday, budget reconciliation conferees eliminated a tax expenditure used to encourage the export of logs at the administration's request. Most of the savings associated with the elimination of tax credit for log exports was earmarked to ensure payments to counties with tax bases that are impacted by the presence of public lands within their borders.

However, I also see that the administration had hoped to use this revenue to fund its northwest economic adjustment initiative for impacted communities and businesses. With the loss of that revenue, the county payments, how does the administration intend to fund this $1.2 billion economic stimulus package?

Mr. Lyons or Mr. Collier.

Mr. COLLIER. As I understand it, Mr. Chairman, last evening, as part of the reconciliation package, language was put in that would guarantee that the so-called owl counties are able to receive or recover funds that they would lose as a result of the reduction of the timber harvest. It looks to us like this language will provide those counties with some $270 million over the next 5 years.

Mr. ROSE. Anything, Mr. Lyons?

Mr. LYONS. That is my understanding, the current status of it, Mr. Chairman.

Mr. ROSE. Thank you. Mr. Studds and then Mr. Lewis.

Mr. VOLKMER. Would the chairman yield just a minute?

Mr. ROSE. Yes, sir.

Mr. VOLKMER. I would just like to take this opportunity—I apologize for being late, but I want to take this opportunity to welcome especially Mr. Lyons, who I worked with on this problem before he got into his present predicament, when he was on staff of the Agriculture Committee—and he has done a tremendous job—and also Dr. Jack Ward Thomas, who I have worked with for quite a few years to bring us to where we are today, and Norm Johnson, two of the "Gang of Four."

I think we all should recognize how far we have gone as far as changing the system of management for the national forest because of the gentlemen who I described and also the rest of the gentlemen at the table.

Thank you, Mr. Chairman.

Mr. ROSE. I thank the gentleman.

Mr. Studds.

Mr. STUDDS. Mr. Chairman, because of the number of members here, so many of whom are from the Northwest, I will forego questions. In some ways, I will observe I feel like I have a personal investment in this process, some programs I should forego even more. I hope you brought in our flack jackets.

I have the impression that even had what you are presenting to us come down from on high on stone tablets, you would still be in receipt of the flack that is about to be incoming or that has already begun from all sides. You have done a remarkable job in an incredibly difficult situation. I commend you and wish you luck. And at least from this perspective, we are here to help you make it work.

I thank the gentleman.

Mr. ROSE. Mr. Lewis.

Mr. LEWIS. I would yield to Mr. Smith of Oregon. Thank you, Mr. Chairman.

Mr. ROSE. Mr. Smith of Oregon is recognized for 5 minutes.

Mr. SMITH of Oregon. Thank you very much, Mr. Chairman. It is interesting to me that we would have three committees and a whole house full of Members of Congress, plus as many as we can get at the witness table, to discuss a very difficult in-depth problem, especially in the Pacific Northwest. One of the reasons that I suppose we are doing that is so that everybody is protected, so I can't lay a glove on you except for 5 minutes, but here it comes with a rock in it.

Mr. Collier, you had some strong and flowery language in your presentation. Governments deliberately wanted to become boxed in, gutting the environmental laws. You agree it is a train wreck. I wonder if that is true. That is an indictment to the agencies of Government that we have professionally managing our timber resource—BLM, Forest Service, in some cases Fish and Wildlife Service—who recommend policies to both agencies.

Are you telling me that these agencies collaborated with some grand conspiracy to deliberately violate the laws of this country and, therefore, if they did, you ought to fire Jack Ward Thomas.

He was part of it, and so is that what you meant when you stated in your statement that there is some sort of conspiracy here?

Mr. COLLIER. Congressman, thank you for giving me the opportunity to clarify what I meant. I stand firmly behind those strong words. I think they are appropriate, but I don't think they are aimed at the professional career members of those agencies.

Just as Judge Dwyer concluded in his opinion when he said this is not the doing of the scientists, foresters, rangers, and others at the working levels of these agencies, it reflects decisions made by higher authorities in the executive branch of Government.

Mr. SMITH of Oregon. Mr. Collier, do you believe that professionals, as they are, protected as Jack Ward Thomas is—you cannot fire him, by the way—protected from any kind of administration, be it Republican or Democrat, do you think they would violate their responsibilities of professionalism in answer to some President who has told them, Jack, go out there and cut more timber than is growing. And if you don't do that, I am going to be mad at you. I can't fire you, but I will be mad at you.

Do you think that is going on? That is what you intimate.

Mr. COLLIER. I think that the policies that were made ignored the recommendations and the science of Jack Ward Thomas. I think if those recommendations and scientific opinions had been followed by the policymakers, we would not be sitting here discussing this matter today.

We would have had an opportunity to deal with the decision at a time when we had much more room to make the appropriate decision, but I stand by the fact that I think the policymakers made the wrong decisions and made them with the wrong intent.

Now, I am not here to point blame today. The only thing I wanted to do was to lay the groundwork for the fact that the reason we were unable to come out with a more attractive plan for the Northwest, to a large extent, had to do with the conduct over the last dozen years.

Mr. SMITH of Oregon. One final follow-up. With my limited time, I want to take advantage of that.

Mr. ROSE. About 1 minute.

Mr. SMITH of Oregon. Thank you, Mr. Chairman.

Is it possible that over the years Congress has been withdrawing land more rapidly than Administrators could cope with it? For instance, prior to this program of the 24 million acres of forested Federal land, 7 million acres had been withdrawn for wilderness, wilds and scenic rivers, et cetera.

Do you think——

Mr. ROSE. I will let him answer the question you have already asked, because we are really out of time and we have a long way to go here.

Mr. Collier, could you quickly answer that?

Mr. SMITH of Oregon. I thought that was a red-cockaded woodpecker.

Mr. ROSE. It is a red-cockaded woodpecker that is in that air vent up there, and as a result, you cannot talk very loud. We have to keep our voices down.

Quickly, please.

Mr. SMITH of Oregon. The point is, we have withdrawn a lot of this land for timber——

Mr. ROSE. No, really, you have asked the only questions you can ask.

Mr. Collier, will you give him an answer, please?

Mr. COLLIER. No.

Mr. ROSE. No is the answer. Thank you.

The gentleman's time has expired.

Mr. Vento is recognized. We have to run this carefully, ladies and gentlemen. We don't have all day.

Mr. VENTO. Yes, thank you, Mr. Chairman, and welcome to our witnesses and the hard work that they have done.

I might say, I could not help in listening to the past exchange, I think the issue here was that policymakers gambled and they lost. They thought they could intimidate the courts and that is why we are where we are today.

And I want to commend you, I think this plan is helpful. I have a lot of questions about it. I am wondering, Mr. Lyons, you invited me to legislate in the last statements of your—the last part of your statement.

Shouldn't we be legislating this plan and putting it in place legislatively if it is a good plan?

Mr. LYONS. Mr. Vento, as you know, having worked together over the years, I must admit that that was the tact I originally believed we should take. However, now on the other side of the dais, and being named in a lawsuit, you get a different perspective on life. I think most importantly, our obligation was to respond to the court, to present a plan that would get us out of the injunction we faced.

I believe that we can implement this plan administratively. It will take some time, it will take cooperation among all the agencies, and it will take some open dialog between the parties in the lawsuit. But I believe we can move forward and implement this strategy, and I believe we can get back to working the woods.

Mr. VENTO. All of us understand the intentions and some of specifics. We are learning about more of the specifics. Now, I know that you have submitted the draft environmental or supplemental environmental impact statement and I want to look at that. But eventually, if this is working and the court relaxes the injunction and it looks like it is going to work, wouldn't it be appropriate at that time, because notwithstanding the policy path we are on today, couldn't this also just lend itself to a further erosion by a decision such as occurred over the last decade that really were detours in terms of sound planning?

Mr. LYONS. The only thing I can assure you, Mr. Vento, is there won't be those detours in this administration, and we will proceed to implement the plan.

Mr. VENTO. I want to get into this 1,400 different species the scientists tried to deal with in terms of the consideration of old-growth related species and principally on a blueprint of watersheds.

The other thing is that in this plan, in the context of watersheds and of those species, I would like you to respond to the need for a GIS information system that you have advocated in your initial presentation to the Congress and to the courts.

Mr. Lyons, if you want to comment, and Dr. Thomas and others at this time for that particular purpose. I want to talk about it in the context of those 1,400 species and the watersheds, which I think is a good route at this time. At least I think it is appropriate.

Mr. LYONS. I will certainly let Jack address some of the technical questions, since he had to go through the workover trying to track down the data necessary to evaluate those species, but I will say this: We have committed to developing an integrated data base in the Pacific Northwest, and this is in fact one of the charges of the interagency team that will be set up in the region.

I think we have come to recognize the difficulties of having inconsistent data bases, of not being able to look at species and resources across geopolitical boundaries or across the boundaries of BLM and Forest Service land, and it has hampered other efforts considerably.

So we are, in fact, committed to developing that unified data base, and we, in fact, are in the process of making what determinations are necessary to gather that information. Clearly, watersheds should be the building block for future planning.

Mr. VENTO. The two devices, watersheds and the 1,400 species, until you develop a GIS, it is the best available information?

Mr. LYONS. It is for now.

Mr. VENTO. One question I wanted to get in, and that is on the memorandum of understanding between the different agencies and departments, what is the status of those and the guidelines that follow them? Can you submit or will you be providing copies of that with the draft supplemental environmental impact statements and/or for the courts? And will we have those in our possession?

Mr. COLLIER. We are very close to finalizing those, Mr. Chairman. Hope to be able to do so here in the next few days. We have not made a decision whether it is necessary to submit those to the court or for public comments. We will be happy to provide the committee with a——

Mr. VENTO. They will be made a part of the record if received in time.

Mr. ROSE. Please try to submit those for the record.

Thank you.

[The material follows:]

31

MEMORANDUM OF UNDERSTANDING

FOR FOREST ECOSYSTEM MANAGEMENT


## I. PARTIES

This is an understanding among five parties:

> The Director of the White House Office on Environmental Policy
> The Secretary of the Interior
> The Secretary of Agriculture
> The Administrator of the Environmental Protection Agency
> The Under Secretary of Commerce for Oceans and Atmosphere


## II. BACKGROUND

The President has proposed a comprehensive plan to alleviate the impasse over management of federal forest lands in the Pacific Northwest within the range of the northern spotted owl. The plan fulfills the President's request for "a balanced and comprehensive strategy for the conservation and management of forest ecosystems, while maximizing economic and social benefits from the forests." By taking an innovative approach based on ecosystem and watershed management, the plan transcends traditional administrative boundaries. Successful implementation will require unprecedented interagency cooperation, coordination, and collaboration, both in the long-term and in the short-term.

The report of the Agency Coordination team established by the President following the April 2, 1993 Forest Conference presents a mechanism to achieve better coordination and cooperation among the federal agencies that are involved in forest management issues. It concluded that "bold changes are required" in how agencies relate to one another and to the states, tribes, private landowners, and communities and people in the region.


## III. PURPOSE

The purpose of this Memorandum of Understanding is to establish a framework for cooperative planning, improved decision making, and coordinated implementation of the forest ecosystem management component of the President's *Forest Plan for a Sustainable Economy and a Sustainable Environment* which is designed to resolve northwest forest issues within the range of the northern spotted owl.

Signatories to this Memorandum of Understanding agree to:

- develop a cohesive vision and shared sense of mission for the management of federal forest lands which balances multiple objectives;

- improve their ability to adapt to change, such as new scientific understanding or changing societal values, in a cohesive manner;

- cultivate greater trust, coordination, and cooperation among federal agencies, within individual agencies, and between federal agencies and non-federal interests;

- address inconsistencies among statutory mandates;

- improve integrated application of agency budgets to maximize efficient use of funds for overlapping or related efforts;

- improve the sharing of information and the pooling of agencies' technology and expertise;

- coordinate ecosystem management activities in concert with federal, state and local programs for economic, labor, and community assistance.

## IV.   STRUCTURE

The following interagency groups are established to develop, monitor, and oversee the implementation of the comprehensive forest management strategy for federal forests within the range of the northern spotted owl. They will support the development and implementation of land and resource management plans. This agreement does not substitute for or alter the line authority of individual agencies.

A. Interagency Steering Committee: The Interagency Steering Committee will establish overall policies governing the prompt, coordinated and effective implementation of the President's forest management plan by all relevant federal agencies and address and resolve issues referred to it by the Regional Executive Committee, described below. The Committee will be located in Washington, D.C. The signatories will appoint representatives to this Committee which will be chaired by the Director of the White House Office on Environmental Policy or her/his designee. A White House appointed representative of the ISC will serve as interagency coordinator to provide general oversight and guidance of regional activities.

B. <u>Regional Interagency Executive Committee (RIEC)</u>: This group will consist of
regional representatives of the agencies signatory to this M.O.U. The chairmanship
of the RIEC will alternate between the Regional Forester and State Director of the
Bureau of Land Management. In appropriate situations this core group will consult
with other federal and state agencies and tribes. The Regional Interagency
Executive Committee will serve as the senior regional entity to assure the prompt,
coordinated and successful implementation of the President's forest management
plan at the regional level. It will serve as the principal conduit for
communications between the Interagency Steering Committee and the region. It
will be responsible for implementing the directives of the Interagency Steering
Committee, reporting regularly on implementation progress, and referring issues
relating to the policies or procedures for implementing the plan to the Interagency
Steering Committee.

The RIEC will appoint an interim interagency implementation team to oversee and
initiate actions during the interim period moving toward to full implementation of
the new forest management strategy.

The Regional Interagency Executive Committee will work together with the Multi-
Agency Command group (MAC) of the Northwest Economic Adjustment Initiatve
to develop criteria and priorities for restoration projects or other ecosystem
investment opportunities.

The Regional Interagency Executive Committee will be accountable to the
Interagency Steering Committee for establishment and oversight of the Regional
Ecosystem Office, Research and Monitoring Committee and Provincial Teams. The
Regional Interagency Executive Committee will also make recommendations for
minimizing planning redundancies.

1.  <u>Regional Ecosystem Office</u>: This office will provide a focal point for
scientific and technical expertise in support of implementation of the forest
management plan. It will also be responsible for evaluation of major
modifications arising from the adaptive management process and will
coordinate the formulation and implementation of data standards. This
office will report to the Regional Interagency Executive Committee and will
be responsible for development, evaluation, and resolution of consistency
and implementation issues with respect to specific topics including, but not
limited to, the following:

    *   Geographic Information Systems
    *   Prototype watershed analyses
    *   Restoration and reforestation guidelines
    *   Support of agency efforts to meet obligations of Endangered
        Species Act (e.g. Section 7 consultations, preparation of recovery
        plans)

- Adaptive management guidelines
- Monitoring
- Research
- Refining definition of reserve boundaries

Agencies will detail staff to the Regional Ecosystem Office as appropriate.

2. Research and Monitoring Committee: This committee, composed of research scientists and managers from a variety of disciplines will provide advice to the Regional Interagency Executive Committee on implementation of the forest plan including adaptive management areas and watershed assessments. The Research and Monitoring Committee will review and evaluate ongoing research, develop a research plan to address critical natural resource commodity and non-commodity questions, and address biological, social, economic, and adaptive management research questions. It will also develop scientifically credible, cost-efficient monitoring plans. The Research and Monitoring Committee will report to the Regional Interagency Executive Committee.

3. Provincial Teams: These teams will consist of representatives of federal agencies, states, tribes, and others. The Interagency Steering Committee and the Regional Interagency Executive Committee will determine the appropriate role for these teams at the level of physiographic provinces, adaptive management areas or particular watersheds.

## V. TERMS

The term of this agreement is five years from the date of execution, after which time the parties may extend the agreement.

AGREED:

_____
Director, White House Office on Environmental Policy


_____
Secretary of the Interior


_____
Secretary of Agriculture


_____
Administrator, Environmental Protection Agency


_____
Under Secretary of Commerce for Oceans and Atmosphere

AGREED:

_____
Director, White House Office on Environmental Policy

_____
Secretary of the Interior

_____
Secretary of Agriculture

_____
Administrator, Environmental Protection Agency

_____
Under Secretary of Commerce for Oceans and Atmosphere

# Forest Ecosystem Management:

## An Ecological, Economic, and Social Assessment

## Report of the Forest Ecosystem Management Assessment Team
### July 1993

United States Department of Agriculture
Forest Service

United States Department of Commerce
National Oceanic and Atmospheric Administration
National Marine Fisheries Service

United States Department of the Interior
Bureau of Land Management

United States Department of the Interior
Fish and Wildlife Service

United States Department of the Interior
National Park Service

Environmental Protection Agency

# Preface

Following the April 2, 1993, Forest Conference in Portland, Oregon, President Clinton created three interagency working groups: the Forest Ecosystem Management Assessment Team, the Labor and Community Assessment Team, and the Agency Coordination Team. Direction for the Teams came in a Statement of Mission letter. The following excerpts from that letter outline the mission for the Forest Ecosystem Management Team.

TO:   **FOREST CONFERENCE INTER-AGENCY WORKING GROUPS**
Ecosystem Management Assessment
Labor and Community Assistance
Agency Coordination

FROM: **FOREST CONFERENCE EXECUTIVE COMMITTEE**

| | |
|---|---|
| Department of Agriculture | Office on Environmental Policy |
| Department of Interior | Office of Science and Technology |
| Department of Labor | National Economic Council |
| Department of Commerce | Council of Economic Advisors |
| Environmental Protection Agency | Office of Management and Budget |

RE:   **STATEMENT OF MISSION**

Together, we are working to fulfill President Clinton's mandate to produce a plan to break the gridlock over federal forest management that has created so much confusion and controversy in the Pacific Northwest and northern California. As well, that mandate means providing for economic diversification and new economic opportunities in the region. As you enter into the critical phase of your work reviewing options and policy, this mission statement should be used to focus and coordinate your efforts. It includes overall guidance and specific guidance for each team.

## BACKGROUND

President Clinton posed the fundamental question we face when he opened the Forest Conference in Portland.

"How can we achieve a balanced and comprehensive policy that recognizes the importance of the forests and timber to the economy and jobs in this region, and how can we preserve our precious old-growth forests, which are part of our national heritage and that, once destroyed, can never be replaced?"

And he said, "The most important thing we can do is to admit, all of us to each other, that there are no simple or easy answers. This is not about choosing between jobs and the environment, but about recognizing the importance of both and recognizing that virtually everyone here and everyone in this region cares about both."

The President said five principles should guide our work:

"First, we must never forget the human and the economic dimensions of these problems. Where sound management policies can preserve the health of forest lands, sales should go forward. Where this requirement cannot be met, we need to do our best to offer new economic opportunities for year-round, high-wage, high-skill jobs.

"Second, as we craft a plan, we need to protect the long-term health of our forests, our wildlife, and our waterways. They are a... gift from God; and we hold them in trust for future generations."

"Third, our efforts must be, insofar as we are wise enough to know it. scientifically sound, ecologically credible, and legally responsible."

"Fourth, the plan should produce a predictable and sustainable level of timber sales and nontimber resources that will not degrade or destroy the environment."

"Fifth, to achieve these goals, we will do our best, as I said, to make the federal government work together and work for you. We may make mistakes but we will try to end the gridlock within the federal government and we will insist on collaboration not confrontation."

## ECOSYSTEM MANAGEMENT ASSESSMENT

Our objectives based on the President's mandate and principles are to identify management alternatives that attain the greatest economic and social contribution from the forests of the region and meet the requirements of the applicable laws and regulations, including the Endangered Species Act, the National Forest Management Act, the Federal Land Policy Management Act, and the National Environmental Policy Act. The Ecosystem Management Assessment working group should explore adaptive management and silvicultural techniques and base its work on the best technical and scientific information currently available.

Your assessment should take an ecosystem approach to forest management and should particularly address maintenance and restoration of biological diversity, particularly that of the late-successional and old-growth forest ecosystems; maintenance of long-term site productivity of forest ecosystems; maintenance of sustainable levels of renewable natural resources, including timber, other forest products, and other facets of forest values; and maintenance of rural economies and communities.

Given the biological requirements of each alternative, you should suggest the patterns of protection, investment, and use that will provide the greatest possible economic and social contributions from the region's forests. In particular, we encourage you to suggest innovative ways federal forests can contribute to economic and social well-being.

You should address a range of alternatives in a way that allows us to distinguish the different costs and benefits of various approaches (including marginal cost/benefit assessments), and in doing so, at least the following should be considered:

- timber sales, short and long term;

- production of other commodities;

# 40

- effects on public uses and values, including scenic quality, recreation, subsistence, and tourism;

- effect on environmental and ecological values, including air and water quality, habitat conservation, sustainability, threatened and endangered species, biodiversity and long-term productivity;

- jobs attributable to timber harvest and timber processing; and, to the extent feasible, jobs attributable to other commodity production, fish habitat protection, and public uses of forests; as well as jobs attributable to investment and restoration associated with each alternative;

- economic and social effects on local communities, and effects on revenues to counties and the national treasury,

- economic and social policies associated with the protection and use of forest resources that might aid in the transitions of the region's industries and communities;

- economic and social benefits from the ecological services you consider;

- regional, national, and international effects as they relate to timber supply, wood product prices, and other key economic and social variables.

As well, when locating reserves, your assessment also should consider both the benefits to the whole array of forest values and the potential cost to rural communities.

The impact of protection and recovery of threatened and endangered species on nonfederal lands within the region of concern should be minimized. However, you should note specific nonfederal contributions that are essential to or could significantly help accomplish the conservation and timber supply objectives of your assessment.

In addition, your assessment should include suggestions for adaptive management that would identify high priority inventory, research, and monitoring needed to assess success over time, and essential or allowable modifications in approach as new information becomes available. You should also suggest a mechanism for a coordinated interagency approach to the needed assessments, monitoring, and research as well as any changes needed in decisionmaking procedures required to support adaptive management.

You should carefully examine silvicultural management of forest stands -- particularly young stands -- especially in the context of adaptive management. The use of silviculture to achieve those ends, or tests of silviculture, should be judged in an ecosystem context and not solely on the basis of single species or several species response.

Your conservation and management assessment should cover those lands managed by the Forest Service, the Bureau of Land Management, and the National Park Service that are within the current range of the northern spotted owl, drawing as you have on personnel from those agencies and assistance from the Fish and Wildlife Service, the National Marine Fisheries Service, and the Environmental Protection Agency. To achieve similar treatment on all federal lands involved here, you should apply the "viability standard" to the Bureau of Land Management lands.

In addressing biological diversity you should not limit your consideration to any one species and, to the extent possible, you should develop alternatives for long-term management that meet the following objectives:

- maintenance and/or restoration of habitat conditions for the northern spotted owl and the marbled murrelet that will provide for viability of each species -- for the owl, well distributed along its current range on federal lands, and for the murrelet so far as nesting habitat is concerned;

- maintenance and/or restoration of habitat conditions to support viable populations, well-distributed across their current ranges, of species known (or reasonably expected) to be associated with old-growth forest conditions;

- maintenance and/or restoration of spawning and rearing habitat on Forest Service, Bureau of Land Management, and National Park Service lands to support recovery and maintenance of viable populations of anadromous fish species and stocks and other fish species and stocks considered "sensitive" or "at risk" by land management agencies, or listed under the Endangered Species Act; and,

- maintenance and/or creation of a connected or interactive old-growth forest ecosystem on the federal lands within the region under consideration.

Your assessment should include alternatives that range from a medium to a very high probability of ensuring the viability of species. The analysis should include an assessment of current agency programs based on Forest Service plans (including the Final Draft Recovery Plan for the Northern Spotted Owl) for the National Forests and the Bureau of Land Management's revised preferred alternative for its lands.

In your assessment, you should also carefully consider the suggestions for forest management from the recent Forest Conference in Portland. Although we know that it will be difficult to move beyond the possibility considered in recent analysis, you should apply your most creative abilities to suggest policies that might move us forward on these difficult issues. You also should address shot-term timber sale possibilities as well as longer term options.

Finally, your assessment should be subject to peer review by appropriately credentialed reviewers.

## CONCLUSION

We appreciate your efforts and recognize, as President Clinton did, that these are difficult issues with difficult choices. And, we'll remind you of something else the President said at the Forest Conference, talking to the people of the Pacific Northwest and northern California: "We're here to begin a process that will help ensure that you will be able to work together in your communities for the good of your businesses, your jobs, and your natural environment. The process we (have begun) will not be easy. Its outcome cannot possibly make everyone happy. Perhaps it won't make anyone completely happy. But the worst thing we can do is nothing."

# Forest Ecosystem Management Assessment Team

**TEAM LEADER**
Jack Ward Thomas

Chief Research Wildlife Biologist, Forest Service, Pacific Northwest Research Station, Forestry and Range Sciences Laboratory, La Grande, Oregon

**DEPUTY TEAM LEADER**
Martin G. Raphael

Principal Research Wildlife Biologist, Forest Service, Pacific Northwest Research Station, Forestry Sciences Laboratory, Olympia, Washington

**TERRESTRIAL ECOLOGY GROUP**
E. Charles Meslow (co-leader)

Research Wildlife Biologist, U.S. Fish and Wildlife Service, Leader, Oregon Cooperative Wildlife Research Unit, and Professor of Wildlife Ecology, Oregon State University, Corvallis, Oregon

Richard S. Holthausen (co-leader)

National Wildlife Ecologist, Forest Service, Pacific Northwest Research Station, Forestry Sciences Laboratory, Corvallis, Oregon

Robert G. Anthony

Assistant Leader, Oregon Cooperative Wildlife Research Unit, U.S. Fish and Wildlife Service, Corvallis, Oregon

Michael W. Collopy

Director of Bureau of Land Management Cooperative Research Unit, Bureau of Land Management, Corvallis, Oregon

Phillip J. Detrich

Supervisory Fish and Wildlife Biologist, U.S. Fish and Wildlife Service, Sacramento Field Office, Sacramento, California

Eric D. Forsman

Research Wildlife Biologist, Forest Service, Pacific Northwest Research Station, Forestry Sciences Laboratory, Corvallis, Oregon

Jerry F. Franklin

Professor of Ecosystem Analysis, College of Forest Resources, University of Washington, Seattle, Washington

Nancy Fredricks

Zone Botanist, Forest Service, Gifford Pinchot National Forest, Carson, Washington

Patricia Greenlee

Threatened and Endangered Species Coordinator, Forest Service, Willamette National Forest, Eugene, Oregon

A. Grant Gunderson — Threatened, Endangered, and Sensitive Species Program Manager, Forest Service, Pacific Northwest Region, Portland, Oregon

Robin Lesher — Botanist, Forest Service, Mount Baker-Snoqualmie National Forest, Seattle, Washington

Joseph B. Lint — State Threatened, Endangered and Sensitive Species Biologist, Bureau of Land Management, Oregon State Office, Portland, Oregon

Bruce G. Marcot — Wildlife Ecologist, Forest Service, Pacific Northwest Research Station, Portland, Oregon

James L. Michaels — Supervisory Fish and Wildlife Biologist, U.S. Fish and Wildlife Service, Olympia, Washington

Gary S. Miller — Fish and Wildlife Biologist, U.S. Fish and Wildlife Service, Portland Field Office, Portland, Oregon

Barry S. Mulder — Project Leader and Spotted Owl Coordinator, Forest Ecosystems Office, U.S. Fish and Wildlife Service, Portland, Oregon

Teresa A. Nichols — Fish and Wildlife Biologist, U.S. Fish and Wildlife Service, Portland Field Office, Portland, Oregon

Charles W. Philpot — Director, Forest Service, Pacific Northwest Research Station, Portland Oregon

Roger Rosentreter — Botanist, Bureau of Land Management, Idaho State Office, Boise, Idaho

David M. Solis — Spotted Owl Program Manager, Forest Service, Pacific Southwest Region, San Francisco, California

Thomas Spies — Research Forester, Forest Service, Pacific Northwest Research Station, Corvallis Forestry Sciences Laboratory, Corvallis, Oregon

Edward E. Starkey — Research Biologist, National Park Service, Cooperative Park Studies Unit, College of Forestry, Oregon State University, Corvallis, Oregon

John C. Tappeiner — Senior Research Forester and Professor, Bureau of Land Management Cooperative Unit, Department of Forest Resources, Oregon State University, Corvallis, Oregon

Cynthia J. Zabel — Project Leader and Research Wildife Biologist, Forest Service, Pacific Southwest Research Station, Redwood Science Laboratory, Arcata, California

## AQUATIC/WATERSHED GROUP

James R. Sedell (co-leader) — Principal Research Ecologist, Forest Service, Pacific Northwest Research Station, Forestry Sciences Laboratory, Corvallis, Oregon

| | |
|---|---|
| Gordon H. Reeves (co-leader) | Research Fish Biologist, Forest Service, Pacific Northwest Research Station, Forestry Sciences Laboratory, Corvallis, Oregon |
| Lisa Brown | Research Assistant, Unclassified, Department of Fish and Wildlife, Oregon State University, Corvallis, Oregon |
| Kelly M. Burnett | Fish Biologist, Forest Service, Pacific Northwest Research Station, Forestry Sciences Laboratory, Corvallis, Oregon |
| John R. Cannell | Forestry Specialist, U.S. Environmental Protection Agency, Washington, D.C. |
| Michael J. Furniss | Watershed Group Leader, Forest Service, Six Rivers National Forest, Eureka, California |
| Elizabeth Holmes Gaar | Chief, Endangered Species Branch, National Marine Fisheries Service, Northwest Region, Portland, Oregon |
| Gordon E. Grant | Research Hydrologist, Forest Service, Pacific Northwest Research Station, Forestry Sciences Laboratory, Corvallis, Oregon |
| R. Dennis Harr | Principal Research Hydrologist, Forest Service, Pacific Northwest Research Station, Forestry Sciences Laboratory, Seattle, Washington |
| Robert House | Anadramous Fish Program Manager, Bureau of Land Management, Boise, Idaho |
| Bruce P. McCannon | Regional Hydrologist, Forest Service, Pacific Northwest Region, Portland, Oregon |
| David R. Montgomery | Research Assistant Professor, Quaternary Research Center, University of Washington, Seattle, Washington |
| Cindy Ricks | Geomorphologist, Forest Service, Siskiyou National Forest, Gold Beach, Oregon |
| Thomas E. Robertson | Water Quality Specialist, U.S. Environmental Protection Agency, Oregon Operations Office, Portland, Oregon |
| Frederick J. Swanson | Principal Research Geologist, Forest Service, Pacific Northwest Research Station, Forestry Sciences Laboratory, Corvallis, Oregon |
| Fred Weimann | Regional Wetland Ecologist, Environmental Protection Agency, Region 10, Seattle, Washington |
| Jack E. Williams | Science Advisor, Office of the Director, Bureau of Land Management, Washington, D.C. |
| Robert R. Ziemer | Principal Research Hydrologist, Forest Service, Pacific Southwest Forest and Range Experiment Station, Redwood Sciences Laboratory, Arcata, California |

## RESOURCE ANALYSIS GROUP

| | |
|---|---|
| K. Norman Johnson (leader) | Professor, Department of Forest Resources, Oregon State University, Corvallis, Oregon |
| Klaus Barber | Systems Analyst, Forest Service, Regional Office, San Francisco, California |
| Sarah Crim | Regional Analyst, Forest Service, Pacific Northwest Region, Portland, Oregon |
| Michael J. Howell, Jr. | Land Information System Coordinator, Bureau of Land Management, Division of Administration, Oregon State Office, Portland, Oregon |
| Richard Phillips | Regional Economist, Forest Service, Pacific Northwest Region, Portland, Oregon |
| Ken Wright | Planning Analyst, Forest Service, Pacific Southwest Region, Six Rivers, California |

## ECONOMIC ASSESSMENT GROUP

| | |
|---|---|
| Brian Greber (leader) | Associate Professor, Forest Resources Economics, College of Forestry, Oregon State University, Corvallis, Oregon |
| Richard Haynes | Economist, Forest Service, Pacific Northwest Research Station, Forestry Sciences Laboratory, Portland, Oregon |
| Cindy Swanson | Economist, Forest Service, Washington Office Wildlife and Fisheries Staff, Washington, DC |

## SOCIAL ASSESSMENT GROUP

| | |
|---|---|
| Roger N. Clark (leader) | RP & A Program Manager, Forest Service, Pacific Northwest Research Station, Seattle, Washington |
| Scott S. Abdon | Recreation Program Leader, Bureau of Land Management, Salem, Oregon |
| Matt Carroll | Assistant Professor, Washington State University, Pullman, Washington |
| Steven Daniels | Associate Professor, Oregon State University, Corvallis, Oregon |
| Sam C. Doak | Resource Policy Analyst, Portland, Oregon |
| Jonathan Kusel | Post-Doctoral Fellow, Univeristy of California, Berkeley, California |
| Ranotta McNair | Nursery Manager, Deschutes National Forest, Bend, Oregon |
| Cynthia Miner | Technological Transfer Specialist, Forest Service, Pacific Northwest Research Station, Portland, Oregon |

| Margaret A. Shannon | Professor of Forest Resources, College of Forest Resources, University of Washington, Seattle, Washington |
|---|---|
| George H. Stankey | Senior Research Professor, Oregon State University, Corvallis, Oregon |
| Victoria Sturtevant | Professor of Sociology, Southern Oregon State College, Ashland, Oregon |
| Ann C. Werner | Social Science Analyst, Oregon State University, Corvallis, Oregon |

## SPATIAL ANALYSIS GROUP

| Duane R. Dippon (co-leader) | ARD/GIS Specialist, Bureau of Land Management, Oregon State Office, Planning, Portland, Oregon |
|---|---|
| John R. Steffenson (co-leader) | Program Manager, Forest Service, Pacific Northwest Region, Geometronics, GIS Analysis Group, Portland, Oregon |
| Anita Bailey | GIS Analyst and GIS Coordinator, Forest Service, Southern Region, Cherokee National Forest, Cleveland, Tennessee |
| Mitchel L. Barton | GIS Analyst and Computer Systems Analyst, Forest Service, Southern Region, Kisatchie National Forest, Pineville, Louisiana |
| Ernie Bergan | Database Analyst and Regional Traffic Engineer, Forest Service, Pacific Northwest Region, Engineering, Portland, Oregon |
| James Blatt | GIS Support and Database Support, Bureau of Land Management, Oregon State Office, GIS Section, on contract from Infotec Development, Portland, Oregon |
| Margo Blosser | GIS Analyst, Bureau of Land Management, Oregon State Office, Planning, ARD/GIS, on contract from Infotec Development, Portland, Oregon |
| Lois Doyle | Map Librarian, Bureau of Land Management, Oregon State Office, GIS Section, Portland, Oregon |
| Theodore W. Falkner | GIS Analyst and GIS Coordinator, Forest Service, Alaska Region, Tongass National Forest, Chatham Area, Sitka, Alaska |
| Beth Galleher | GIS Analyst, Forest Service, Pacific Northwest Research Station, Forestry Sciences Laboratory, Olympia, Washington |
| Mathew L. Gilson | GIS Technician, Forest Service, Pacific Northwest Region, Geometronics, GIS Analysis Group, Portland, Oregon |

| | |
|---|---|
| Becky Gravenmier | GIS Analyst/Quality Control and GIS Specialist, Bureau of Land Management, Oregon State Office, GIS Section, Portland, Oregon |
| Rick S. Griffen | GIS Analyst and Resource Information Manager, Forest Service, Alaska Region, Tongass National Forest, Tongass Land Management Plan Revision Team, Juneau, Alaska |
| Loc Hoang | Database Analyst, Bureau of Land Management, Oregon State Office, GIS Section, on contract from Infotec Development, Portland, Oregon |
| Julie L. Johnson | GIS Analyst and GIS Coordinator, Forest Service, Pacific Northwest Region, Forest Pest Management, Portland, Oregon |
| Terry Locke | Database Analyst, Bureau of Land Management, Oregon State Office, GIS Section, on contract from Infotec Development, Portland, Oregon |
| Virginia Lutz | GIS Analyst and Computer Assistant, Forest Service, Alaska Region, Tongass National Forest, Chatham Area, Sitka, Alaska |
| Janet L. McCormick | GIS Analyst and GIS Specialist, Forest Service, Pacific Northwest Region, Geometronics, GIS Analysis Group, on contract from Infotec Development, Portland, Oregon |
| Arthur Miller | Database Analyst, Bureau of Land Management, Oregon State Office, GIS Section, on contract from Infotec Development, Portland, Oregon |
| Michael Moscoe | Documentation and Management Analyst, Bureau of Land Management, Oregon State Office, GIS Section, Portland, Oregon |
| Charlene L. Neihardt | GIS Analyst and Hydrologist, Forest Service, Southern Region, Ouachita National Forest, Hot Springs, Arkansas |
| A. Paul Newman | GIS Analyst and GIS/Remote Sensing Specialist, Forest Service, Pacific Northwest Region, Geometronics, GIS Analysis Group, on contract from Pacific Meridian Resources, Portland, Oregon |
| Jeffery S. Nighbert | GIS Analyst and Senior Technical Specialist, Bureau of Land Management, Oregon State Office, GIS Section, Portland, Oregon |
| Steve Salas | GIS Analyst, Bureau of Land Management, Oregon State Office, GIS Section, on contract from Infotec Development, Portland, Oregon |
| Douglas C. Taylor | GIS Technician, Forest Service, Pacific Northwest Region, Geometronics, GIS Analysis Group, Portland, Oregon |

| | |
|---|---|
| Richard Van de Water | GIS Analyst, Forest Service, Pacific Southwest Region, Klamath National Forest, Yreka, California |
| Robert Varner | Database Analyst and Engineering Systems Analyst, Forest Service, Pacific Northwest Region, Portland, Oregon |
| Margaret Watry | Database Administrator and Resource Information Specialist, Forest Service, Pacific Northwest Region, Management Systems, Planning Group, Portland, Oregon |
| William Wettengel | GIS Analyst, Forest Service, Pacific Northwest Region, Olympic National Forest, Olympia, Washington |
| Michelle R. Widener | GIS Analyst and Geographer, Forest Service, Southern Region, George Washington National Forest, Harrisonburg, Virginia |
| Andrew E. Wilson | GIS Technical Coordinator and Senior GIS Analyst, Forest Service, Pacific Northwest Region, Geometronics, GIS Analysis Group, Portland, Oregon |
| John A. Young | GIS Analyst and Geographer/GIS Coordinator, Forest Service, Pacific Northwest Research Station, Forestry Sciences Laboratory, Olympia, Washington |

## SUPPORT
### Administration

| | |
|---|---|
| Nancy F. DeLong (Administrative Officer) | Telecommunications Manager, Forest Service, Umatilla National Forest, Pendleton, Oregon |
| Robert T. Jacobs (Group Leader) | Supplemental Environmental Impact Statement Team Leader, Deputy Regional Forester, Forest Service, Pacific Northwest Region, Portland, Oregon |
| Linda A. Kucera (Facilitator and Document Preparation) | Information and Education Assistant, U.S. Fish and Wildlife Service, Region 1, Regional Office, Ecological Services, Portland, Oregon |
| Kaydonna Pennell (SEIS Administrative Officer) | Management Assistant, Pacific Northwest Region, Portland, Oregon |
| Delbert E. Thompson (Visual Information Specialist) | Pacific Northwest Research Station, Forest Service, Portland, Oregon |
| Alexandria R. Walker (Administrative Assistant) | Executive Secretary, Forest Service, Pacific Northwest Research Station, Station Director's Office, Portland, Oregon |

### Editor

| | |
|---|---|
| D. Louise Kingsbury | Supervisory Technical Publications Editor, Forest Service, Intermountain Research Station, Ogden, Utah |

# Forest Ecosystem Management:

# An Ecological, Economic, and Social Assessment

## Table of Contents

# Chapter I

# EXECUTIVE SUMMARY

Timber cutting and other operations on lands managed by the Forest Service and the Bureau of Land Management within the range of the northern spotted owl have been brought virtually to a halt by federal court orders. As a result, the Administration commissioned the Forest Ecosystem Management Assessment Team to formulate and assess the consequences of an array of management options that might form the basis of a solution to the crisis. The Team was told that the objectives were to produce management alternatives that would comply with existing laws and produce the highest contribution to economic and social well being.

The effort reported here is conceived as Phase I of a multiphased approach to ecosystem management. In this first phase, the "backbone" for ecosystem management for the federal forests within the range of the northern spotted owl is, in varying combinations, constructed of a network of late-successional forests and an interim and long-term scheme for protection of aquatic and associated riparian habitats adequate to provide for threatened species and "at risk" species associated with such habitats. In subsequent phases it is expected that planning will be carried out that extends ecosystem management concepts to multiple federal ownerships and, perhaps, to state and private lands (at the discretion of those landholders).

The Team was comprised of scientists and technical experts of a variety of disciplines from the Forest Service, Bureau of Land Management, Environmental Protection Agency, U.S. Fish and Wildlife Service, National Park Service, National Marine Fisheries Service, and from several universities. Over 600 scientists, technicians, and support personnel contributed in some fashion to this effort.

Some 48 previously prepared options addressing the issues of conservation of threatened species (spotted owls and marbled murrelets), anadromous fish, and the late-successional/old-growth ecosystems were examined and evaluated. Using the principles put forward in these previous exercises, 10 additional options were developed and analyzed. These options encompassed various mixtures of Late-Successional Reserves, Riparian Reserves, and prescriptions for the management of the forest both inside and outside of reserves. Most management would occur in areas outside of reserves, called the Matrix. The sizing, spacing, and silvicultural activities allowed in reserves varied between options. The size of the reserves varied from 4.2 to 11.5 million acres.

In one option, there is provision for 10 Adaptive Management Areas arrayed across the landscape and ranging from 84,000 to 400,000 acres. Their purpose is to provide areas where managers can use innovative approaches, perhaps at a landscape scale, to achieve management objectives. These areas will also provide a laboratory for innovative social mechanisms for managing federal lands and areas of mixed ownerships in a more cooperative and interactive fashion. These Adaptive Management Areas could be incorporated into any option presented, with some modification and additional assessment.

For each of the 10 options, the Team evaluated the likelihood of maintaining well-distributed habitat conditions on the federal lands for threatened marbled murrelets and northern spotted owls. In addition, for seven of the options, similar assessments were done for over 1,000 plant and animal species thought to be closely associated with late-successional forests. The likelihood of maintaining a connected viable late-successional ecosystem was also evaluated. These likelihoods varied across options but, in general, were found to be directly related to the amount of late-successional forest in reserve status. These results were reported without comment as to whether they met the statutory requirements of the Endangered Species Act or the regulations issued pursuant to the National Forest Management Act.

At-risk fish species and stocks were similarly assessed, and the ratings seemed most sensitive to the degree of stream side/watershed protection afforded. Such assessments for the northern spotted owl and marbled murrelet resulted in eight of 10 options having a likelihood of achieving habitat conditions suitable to maintain viable populations well distributed on the federal lands. Of the 10 options for at-risk fish species or stocks, eight would result in a reversal of the trend of habitat degradation on federal lands and begin a process of recovery of the aquatic ecosystems on those lands. The Team conducted the most thorough assessment to date of the "viability" of the broad array of species associated with late-successional forest conditions. There were numerous problems in trying to evaluate "real world" biological conditions against the language in the regulations issued pursuant to the National Forest Management Act.

Probable annual sale quantity estimates were completed for each option and compared to harvest levels for the period 1980 through 1989 (4.6 billion board feet per year) and 1990 through 1992 (2.4 billion board feet per year). The anticipated sale level, including cull and salvage volume, ranged from 0.2 billion board feet per year to 1.8 billion board feet per year across the options.

Nonfederal timber harvests have historically accounted for two-thirds of the harvest in the region. Nonfederal timber harvests seem likely to respond to higher prices in the 1990's, resulting in cutting above the sustained yield levels at a rate of 9.4 billion to 9.8 billion board feet per year. In aggregate, timber harvested and processed from all owners is projected to be some 0.8 billion to 2.1 billion board feet (7 to 17 percent) less than the 1990 through 1992 level and 3.5 billion to 4.7 billion board feet (24 to 32 percent) less than the levels of the 1980's, depending on the option.

Direct timber industry employment was as high as 152,000 as recently as 1988. It was approximately 144,900 in 1990 and dropped to an estimated 125,400 in 1992. The employment level anticipated for the next decade varies from 112,900 to 125,000 across the options.

State level forecasts for Oregon and Washington indicate that the aggregate economy will continue to grow regardless of the option chosen. The Washington outlook is rather stable while Oregon's economy is poised to expand 7.4 to 8.7 percent in the aggregate, between 1992 and 1995.

Large-scale reductions are expected in federal receipts and shares to local counties. Unless Congress continues to provide a "safety net," local government revenues could decline by $147 million to $277 million from the 1990 through 1992 level of $294 million, depending on the option.

Consequences to communities vary by option and by rural community. Community capacity to accommodate to change seems to be the most important factor in a community's anticipated ability to adjust to lowered federal timber harvest levels. Those communities that are dependent for federal timber supply and have low capacity to adjust are those communities most at risk. Some communities have already suffered severe impact from reduced timber supply and will suffer even more under most – probably all – of the options developed. Suggestions are made as to how help may be provided to those communities during a period of transition.

We describe a possible and detailed scenario for carrying out a phased coordinated and collaborative movement to achievement of ecosystem management for the federal lands within the range of the northern spotted owl. It is obvious that a new approach to coordinated and collaborative government (i.e., interagency) activities is essential if there is to be speedy recovery from the current impasse. Suggestions are made as to how that might be achieved so that momentum may not be lost as the implementation of a preferred option for ecosystem management proceeds.

We have done our best to fulfill the charge given to us in the time allotted. We believe the assessments of the current situation, the previous assessments of the situation, and the options presented herein are adequate to support an informed decision as to a course of action. Our work as scientists, economists, analysts, and technicians is complete. Whatever decisions that may emerge from this work are now, most appropriately, in the hands of elected leaders.

(The complete report is held in the committee files.)

Mr. VENTO. Mr. Chairman, I would yield back the balance of my time.

Mr. ROSE. Thank you, sir.

Mr. Lewis of Florida to recognize members on his side.

Mr. LEWIS. Yield 5 minutes to Mr. Taylor from North Carolina.

Mr. ROSE. Mr. Taylor.

Mr. TAYLOR of North Carolina. Mr. Chairman.

You know, Mr. Collier, you say you are not here to place blame, but you sound an awful lot like the son who has killed his father and is coming here to plead for mercy and understanding on the basis of being an orphan.

The whole Byzantine labyrinth of laws and regulations that have been based mostly on hysteria and political drive rather than science are what is the foundation for the plan.

You said one of your first orders was from the President to follow the law; then you were pretty much locked in to what you have. I am not sure whether you could have gotten to any other position if you followed that course.

What I am disappointed with, and I hope we can convince this administration, because I think there are good people in the administration, is that they did not begin where they should, and that is with the comprehensive review of the labyrinth of environmental laws and regulations that have been put together. Many of these laws were based on myth and hysteria which evolved into public policy, and now we are basing the next course of action on those foolish decisions made in the past.

I am disappointed that we have not considered the grave environmental damage that is going to be done with the decisions we are making now, and there are surely a number of environmental problems we are going to suffer. We have not looked at that based on the decisions.

We have to have alternatives to what we are doing now.

What I would ask, in the short remaining time, is that in putting the study together, did you consider the minimum amount of timber for the basic infrastructure, especially for components of that infrastructure that bring about the best silviculture methods?

Did you look at the inventory necessary or the minimal inventory necessary, the minimal cutting amount necessary, to utilize the scientific harvest methods that we have now?

And second, when you were setting aside watershed areas, were the soil side indexes of the species' composition in those areas matched against what we are retaining, what we are not cutting?

Mr. LYONS. I will address that, Mr. Taylor. Being a forester such as yourself, you know how complex silviculture is and what tools we have at our disposal. I think what is exciting actually about this plan is that it seeks to use many more of the tools than we have used in the past.

The traditional approach to management in the Pacific Northwest has been to use clearcutting for silviculture, which then leads to planting and regeneration of those forest stands. We have, in this plan, sought to use a wider range of silvicultural tools and to try and manage the woods in a manner that yields timber but also recognizes that other management objectives, multiuse management objectives can be achieved in management of the matrix.

We are going to try and use a much broader array of tools. Having data on how much old growth is out there, having some better understanding, the relationship between how we cut and what impact it has on resources is something we need to learn more about.

Mr. TAYLOR of North Carolina. But in making the plan, did you do a study of the basic, minimum amount necessary for infrastructure survival? Especially a certain component of that, components that we have developed that really are very friendly to the environment and now may be lost because of the plan that you are putting forth?

Mr. LYONS. I am not clear on that in terms of components, Mr. Taylor.

Mr. TAYLOR of North Carolina. Let me give you an example, and we are not talking about just the Pacific Northwest here. We are talking about the whole Nation ultimately. There is now a Pacific Northwest in everybody's future. When you look at what we have done in the Appalachian area, we have developed skyline logging in order to keep down road construction in the steeper areas and to utilize the best silviculture. The demonstrations and pressures by many groups stopped any activity, cut the minimum harvest so none of the skyline logging operations could be used. Now we are losing those components, and if this area is ever logged, it is going to have to be with the most disastrous type for the environment.

Mr. ROSE. The gentleman's time has expired. I thank him for his statement and his questions, and Mr. Lyons if you will please send an answer to Mr. Taylor's office, we thank you. Mr. Miller is recognized for 5 minutes.

Mr. MILLER. Thank you, Mr. Chairman, and I think that we would all prefer that this group and the original "Gang of Four" had many more options available to them when they were in the process of trying to advise us what the possibilities were for a modern and sustainable forest policy. But the fact is, Mr. Smith, that the record is replete with efforts made time and again to overrule the scientists, to disregard reviews of various studies that were sending up warning signals time and again over the last decade, that documented the trouble that these forests were getting themselves into because of the mismanagement—basically the political mismanagement—of these forests.

The last time I was in this hearing room was a joint hearing where the Forest Service was put on notice by its own scientists as to fish studies and the problems that the ASQ driven timber harvests were causing. Their review of that fish study was politely ignored, deep-sixed by the higher echelons that wanted to continue to drive the cutting of this forest.

Time and again, when foresters on the ground said that timber was not available, or that reforesting was not successful, we saw that those warnings were ignored by the politicians who wanted to continue to drive a larger timber harvest. Now, tragically, that practice p us in the situation of making all of the options far more difficult, not just for the industry but for the communities and the economies and the people who work in this industry.

That part of this equation cannot be ignored. It cannot be denied; it is on the record, and the GAO and the Inspector General's office throughout the agencies responsible for the management of these forests over the last decade. That is what brings us to this point today.

Sure, this President would have loved to have had a whole range of additional options. They weren't available. They were cut down. Sure you would have had options about watersheds that maybe you could have lightly touched. They weren't available. They were already too heavily touched.

Sure you would have liked to have believed that you had second growth coming behind the current harvest practices from actions we took 15 and 20 years ago. They are not there. They don't exist. They were overrated. They were put into the count when they didn't in fact exist. So today we don't have those options.

What we do have is this plan, to try to have a resolution of that problem so we can get back to those forests and the other resources within those forests on a sustainable basis.

If I might just have one question, and that is the concern I have with the adaptive management areas. The largest I believe is in California, and my concern goes to the management of those areas. It spans two forests that include many of the resources and the values that we encompass in the ecosystem approach.

Who is it that is going to have some say about assuring a balance in the development of those special management areas as you envision them? Because there are obviously going to be competing interests, strong competing interests at the local level.

Mr. LYONS. Let me give you a short answer to that, Mr. Chairman, and then I will ask Jerry Franklin to give you the long answer. But the short answer is that those areas will be managed to achieve the same management objectives in the President's plan.

The difference is, within those adaptive management areas, we want to foster experimentation, we want to foster the development of local solutions to achieving those same management objectives. The same opportunities for public input to the planning process will exist, however, we want to encourage local involvement and local participation in making those decisions so people feel more empowered to be able to——

Mr. MILLER. We have a mechanism to ensure there is a balance between those local interests. In many of those local areas there is not exactly a balance. They haven't kept in mind that they would have a balanced approach to this so that they could then develop these forests in the future.

Mr. LYONS. That is clearly our objective, to have that kind of balance advisory input.

Mr. MILLER. Thank you, and Jerry's response can be sent to my office. I think those are important innovative provisions that you have brought to this plan, and I would just like to thank you, and especially to thank the scientists for the incredible number of hours that you have given to the solution to this problem. Unfortunately, for the most part, politicians were not willing to engage in making the kinds of tough political policy decisions that needed to be made, and I think that you have just given outstanding service to this country.

Mr. ROSE. Thank you very much, Mr. Miller. Mr. Lewis, is recognized on his side.

Mr. LEWIS. Mr. Herger from California, for 5 minutes.

Mr. HERGER. Thank you very much, Mr. Chairman. Mr. Collier, I have to commend you. I don't know if I have ever heard a more eloquent delivery and testimony than you have presented before these subcommittees. Within that testimony, you mentioned several times balance, and I would like to just point something out to you.

I represent a district in northern California that has parts or all of some seven national forests within it. As of last August, our regional forester indicated that at that time, somewhere between 70 and 80 percent of the forests in all of California, including my district, were off limits to any type of harvesting of timber, which meant that at that time we only had 20, the 25 percent of this pie that we had to work on to be able to supply our Nation with the wood products and paper products that it so dearly needs.

My district has some 27 mills that have closed in the last several years. I have unemployment in one of my counties as high as 21 percent. We have an alternative nine included in what you and our President indicates as being a balanced plan which cuts that limited pie back another 70 percent.

I have a question—I just want to make a statement really, that the citizens of my northern California district, and I suspect all of Oregon and Washington as well, feel it is not balanced, that your plan is a total disaster and is anything but balanced.

I do have a question. My question is really for you, Mr. Lyons, if you would, and in just follow-up of this. We know that as we come south from Washington to Oregon into northern California into my area, the climate changes, we come into more mild winters, not as much rainfall as we have to the north of us, therefore our forests are legitimately, as pointed out by all our scientists, very unique, and in a number of different areas.

One, we have a lot more owls than any other place. We found some four times more owls than they thought they had when they listed in 1990. My question is, is that, was this unique—as a matter of fact, even, Mr. Thomas, and we have spent a number of conversations together, Mr. Jack Ward Thomas indicated even at the time I believe, I want to make sure I am quoting you right, there were some misunderstandings evidently, but that I believe you felt there was a case to be made of perhaps not listing the spotted owl in northern California at the time that it was listed; is that correct?

Mr. J. THOMAS. When I was chairman of the Interagency Scientific Committee, the listing team from the Fish and Wildlife Service was working simultaneously with us. We were asked to make input into that plan. We said that they might want to consider the situation in northern California, particularly that which existed on private land in making their decision and they might want to consider listing by section of the country.

Mr. HERGER. Thank you very much. That is basically what I was trying to say. Mr. Lyons, my question to you is twofold. One, was the uniqueness of northern California considered in this plan which all of you call as being balanced?

Mr. LYONS. I am going to let Dr. Thomas address that specifically, Mr. Herger. Let me just say one thing quickly. It is important to recognize that, particularly for northern California and for the BLM districts, that this plan used as a starting point to draft forest plans that have been prepared in those areas. That was the anchor in essence for the development of option 9 and additional modifications were necessary to achieve some of the management objectives so that uniqueness is reflected.

Mr. HERGER. That wasn't my question. Was it considered in—my question to you I believe, for all practical purposes, it was not considered and I would like to make a formal request of you now, Mr. Lyons, that you and the President and this administration would consider that, would make a new study in that area to consider the uniqueness.

For example, I had some 400,000 acres of forest burn in 1987. The concern is is that the plan that we have, we will see more of our forests burn up rather than be managed.

Mr. ROSE. I thank the gentleman for his question.

Mr. HERGER. Is the answer a yes on that?

Mr. LYONS. I would encourage, Mr. Herger, that since we are in a public comment process, that that kind of information be made a part of the review of the proposed offering.

Mr. HERGER. Is that a no, that you would not study it again?

Mr. ROSE. The gentleman's time has expired. Please submit a better answer if you would like to Mr. Herger.

Mr. DeFazio.

Mr. HERGER. Mr. Chairman, I am asking you to at least allow a yes or a no.

Mr. ROSE. He said he didn't have a yes or no. The gentleman is out of order. I would like to recognize my colleague now. Mr. DeFazio is recognized for 5 minutes.

Mr. DEFAZIO. Thank you, Mr. Chairman. My district is the most impacted. I have a lot of questions. I will go fast, and I will ask the witnesses to please respond as briefly as possible so we can get through a few things here.

First off, Mr. Lyons stated substantial relief from restrictions on private land in the region are anticipated. Further, as I read the report, it anticipates that there will not only be status quo on private lands, but in fact an acceleration of harvest. That is on page II–52 of the report, an increase up to 9.4, 9.8 billion, Dr. Johnson. What inventories and assumptions did you use to reach that and if you can answer quickly? There has been an extraordinary acceleration in harvest on private lands. How is that going to be maintained?

And second, in the promulgation of a 4(d) rule or other restrictions, what assumptions did you make there in terms of restrictions on private land harvest?

Mr. JOHNSON. Congressman DeFazio, I estimated the harvest on Federal land but Brian Greber did it for private land.

Mr. DEFAZIO. OK, quick, Dr. Greber.

Mr. GREBER. If you look at those increases, it ends up being a 1.5-percent increase on non-Federal lands over the level of the 1980's. So it was not a rapidly escalating harvest that was assumed. We used the most——

Mr. DEFAZIO. If you look at what is going on out in Oregon, there has been great concern expressed over the fact that we are harvesting immature trees, trees that are being harvested while they are still lower than meeting annual increment in addition to their volume. You are assuming we are going to continue this extraordinary harvest?

Mr. GREBER. No. It is not a sustainable harvest level and by the year 2000 it drops down substantially.

Mr. DEFAZIO. What assumptions did you make in terms of restrictions on private land regarding the 4(d) rule or other restrictions?

Mr. GREBER. The restrictions that were modeled would primarily parallel what current State forest practices would be.

Mr. DEFAZIO. So you assume no restrictions with the 4(d) rule.

Now, Mr. Collier, my understanding is Fish and Wildlife is in the process of promulgating a 4(d) rule. I further understand that in promulgating that rule, the rumors are it will fall much more heavily on interspersed ownership, small ownerships as much in Oregon than it will in large ownerships in Washington State, particularly large industrial ownerships. Is that true?

Mr. COLLIER. I will get a report on the status of that rule this afternoon, Congressman, but it would not surprise me if your characterization isn't correct.

Mr. DEFAZIO. So then your assumption is faulty, Mr. Greber, because as these restrictions fall, then that timber won't be available for harvest.

Now, if we take that a little bit further and we look at the 4(d) rule that—Dr. Franklin, when I look at the BLM lands, I see we have some very large reserves that are every other section. Every other section of those large reserves is private land in Oregon. We are hearing that in all probability there will be restrictions placed on those private lands. My understanding is that this whole plan is based on the assumption that there will be no additional restriction on those lands. We just heard that the harvest levels are based on that.

Would that not be inconsistent to say on the one hand we drew up these restrictions on the Federal lands assuming private lands would go ahead unfettered. Then you come back and restrict the private lands but still have those restrictions on those Federal lands, particularly the interspersed ownerships.

Mr. FRANKLIN. Congressman, that is really not an appropriate question for me, but your logic is there and I think the administration is working on a resolution of that. Obviously if you provide for it one place——

Mr. DEFAZIO. That could do. To Mr. Collier, Mr. Collier, your boss, Secretary Babbitt has told us the administration is going to provide 2 billion board feet of timber next year. Can you break that down for me?

Mr. COLLIER. I believe that is a combination of two things. It is 1 billion that has already been sold that is out there.

Mr. DEFAZIO. Are you going to review that, whether it is operable?

Mr. COLLIER. Yes.

Mr. DEFAZIO. So some portion of that will fall out?

Mr. COLLIER. I think that is our best estimate of what we think will not fall out, Congressman.

Mr. DEFAZIO. BLM and Forest Service previously?

Mr. COLLIER. Yes, sir.

Mr. DEFAZIO. How are you going to pay the damages on the part you are not going to allow to go forward?

Mr. COLLIER. We are still looking at that.

Mr. DEFAZIO. Where is the rest?

Mr. COLLIER. The rest is from new sales that are prepared to go forward. We hope we can get out from under the injunction.

Mr. DEFAZIO. How are you going to get out from under the injunction to sell the new sales?

Mr. COLLIER. I am sitting here with a letter from the plaintiffs from that action where they have committed to us to work together to identify a volume of timber and to join us in a joint motion to the court to allow that to go forward notwithstanding the injunctions. I have been negotiating that.

Mr. DEFAZIO. So you are looking at 1 billion board feet of new sale?

Mr. COLLIER. Right now only looking at 200 million in the first phase and I don't know where we are going to go from there.

Mr. DEFAZIO. So we have 1 billion preexisting, 200 million new. Where is the other 800 million?

Mr. COLLIER. There are a couple of places we can look to. The original estimate was 1 billion in new sales we hope to get through during the course of a year from the announcement of the President's plan.

Mr. DEFAZIO. Time is up.

Mr. ROSE. Mr. Baesler.

Mr. BAESLER. I would like to yield my 5 minutes to him.

Mr. ROSE. Beg your pardon?

Mr. BAESLER. If Mr. DeFazio would wish, I would like to yield my 5 minutes to him. He knows more about it than I do.

Mr. DEFAZIO. Well, thank you.

Mr. ROSE. Mr. Baesler yields his time to Mr. DeFazio.

Mr. DEFAZIO. So I can then finish up a little bit, Mr. Collier, quickly. So you expect 1 billion of preexisting sales will not be restricted and somehow they are going to pay damages and buy back those others. 200 million of new on BLM and Forest Service, and are we still talking about this mythical 500 million coming from Indian lands?

Mr. COLLIER. That is in there also, Congressman.

Mr. DEFAZIO. Just my reflection, some of the most despoiled lands I have seen on the face of the Earth like the whole Indian reservation. I can't imagine this 500 million of sustainable timber harvest out there on those Indian lands.

I would hope we are not pressuring them into doing something to reach this goal that would not be wise. I have been very concerned since the first time I heard that. OK, where is the other 200? We are getting there.

Mr. COLLIER. We are getting close, and there is some more that I hope will be a phase 2 in terms of getting it out from under the injunction, Congressman.

Mr. DEFAZIO. OK.

Mr. COLLIER. The Indian timber is not sustainable by the way. We think we got 500 in backlog that we can——

Mr. DEFAZIO. Mr. Greber, on your job loss estimates, you assumed, one, that 1.2 billion would be available next year. I assume—my assumption is—the way I read it—is the 1.2 billion was new, not 1.2 billion of preexisting sold contracts that were currently operable under the court orders.

Mr. GREBER. Two quick things. No job loss estimates. We did job projections. Those job losses depend on your choice of baseline. So my job projections were based upon 1.2 billion board foot, and that is once the plan is implemented.

If there is something that delays that 1.2 billion, the employment level would be lower than that. If there are increased levels of harvest permitted in some way, they would be higher than that. That is the level once the plan is in existence.

Mr. DEFAZIO. If we are seeing that some of the existing—some of the existing contracts would be not operable as he has just told us they will not be?

Mr. GREBER. The only assumption is once the plan is in place, if it generates this volume of sales and those sales are harvested, that would be the employment. The transition to that is not discussed in the economic analysis.

Mr. DEFAZIO. So you are saying these are a projection of sustainable jobs then. So if the 1.2 billion is not available next year and we are hearing it likely will not be, how many—let's say that number is zero. How many more jobs are lost?

Mr. GREBER. If the number drops to zero?

Mr. DEFAZIO. Yes.

Mr. GREBER. You would probably be looking at an additional 7,000 to 8,000 jobs.

Mr. DEFAZIO. I understand you assume no losses in pulp and paper. Why? Quickly.

Mr. GREBER. Complicated answer. Pulp and paper sector——

Mr. DEFAZIO. Maybe you could provide that for the record then if it is a complicated answer, but I would really like to know the answer why we assume that since I am hearing from pulp and paper folks—in fact, I have one closed down just this week. It has to do with both price and availability and the price obviously stays high as timber is not available.

You are assuming this nonsustainable private land harvest you already told us, that is correct, in order to reach these numbers of projections?

Mr. GREBER. Right.

Mr. DEFAZIO. And then no indirect job losses. I had this discussion with Mr. Yew. Would you please tell me how a county like Douglas County, where there is 80 percent or 70 percent, I think, according to the State of total dependents on the timber industry for their whole economy, how you do not have any indirect job losses in Douglas County, quickly?

Mr. GREBER. We never stated that there were not indirect job losses. We reported that there are 1.12 indirect and induced jobs per timber industry job, but we pointed out that a lot of those could represent lost opportunities. So rather than doing a static with and without comparison, we did job forecast.

Mr. DEFAZIO. If we go next year and you said 6,000, we lost 6,000 more if we don't sell the 1.2 billion, and then the indirect at

1.2, then it sounds to me like we are looking at instead of 6,000 jobs lost or not available or foregone opportunities, however the economists want to put it, you are talking about 12 plus 1.2, times 12 which takes us up to about 25,000 jobs. Is that accurate?

Mr. GREBER. I would not say that all those indirect and induced effects would represent jobs that are lost.

Mr. DEFAZIO. They are just people who are not working?

Mr. GREBER. A portion of them are people that would lose their jobs. A portion of them are jobs that would not be created in the economy.

Mr. DEFAZIO. What percentage of this total job impact falls in southwest Oregon, as you understand it? Lane, Douglas, and Linn Counties.

Mr. GREBER. Of the timber industry job impacts, roughly two-thirds.

Mr. DEFAZIO. Two-thirds, thank you.

Mr. ROSE. The gentleman's time is expired.

Mr. Lewis.

Mr. LEWIS. Yield 5 minutes to Mr. Goodlatte of Virginia.

Mr. GOODLATTE. Thank you.

Mr. Collier and Mr. Lyons, very quickly, earlier this year the administration proposed shutting down commercial timber sales on 58 primarily eastern forests, including two in my congressional district, which would effectively reduce the market by an additional 3 billion board feet.

What effect does your proposed policy here have on that proposal? Is that going to change that plan by the administration?

Mr. LYONS. Congressman, they are really unrelated issues because we are in fact not going to be shutting down any below-cost forests. What I have committed to is a complete analysis of the timber sale program to make a determination as to how to proceed to implement a below-cost timber sales policy.

We fully expect to operate those sales, and as I said, it was false information that was circulated that 58 forests would be shut down as a result of implementing that policy.

Mr. GOODLATTE. I am encouraged by that.

Mr. Chairman, I yield the balance of my time to Mr. Smith of Oregon.

Mr. SMITH of Oregon. I thank the gentleman indeed for yielding his remaining time to me. I have here before me a timber sale time line dated June 30, 1993, which indicates the time line that the Bureau of Land Management and the Forest Service might be able to get to the point of harvest of any new sales.

The BLM date is March 1, 1995. The Forest Service date is September 16, 1994. Now, you just told us that there is going to be 1 billion of new sales if you can get the issue by Judge Dwyer lifted. How can we possibly have any timber available at all if these time lines are followed?

Mr. COLLIER. Congressman, those time lines were prepared at my request by my staff seeking a worst case analysis of what would happen if things were done the way they had been done in the past.

We then took that as a starting point and made some different decisions on how to proceed. One of the most significant decisions we made is that there is no reason to wait to lay out green sales until January of next year when the plan has finally come out of the process that the court has set in motion.

In other words, we can start laying out those green sales tomorrow or yesterday, as we have done.

Mr. SMITH of Oregon. Sorry, Mr. Collier. You understand that this time line begins on April 2, 1993 from BLM.

Mr. COLLIER. I appreciate that.

Mr. SMITH of Oregon. And April 2, 1993 for the Forest Service.

Mr. COLLIER. It is also a time line that takes each of the significant steps and deals with them consecutively and does not attempt to deal with the process in parallel fashion where it is appropriate.

That is the time line we have now done and that is the time line we are talking about today, and it allows us to be in a process, we believe, to have new green sales on the ground for the Forest Service next year, early in the year, and we think that is something that we can accommodate, and the way you accommodate is take that time line you got and rip it in half and put the pieces parallel, and you will see that two of those processes can run at the same time.

There is no reason that you have to run them consecutively as they have done in the past.

Mr. SMITH of Oregon. Assuming no litigation, assuming no critical habitat for marbled murrelet?

Mr. COLLIER. Congressman, not assuming no litigation. Litigation can proceed parallel also. Assuming that we do not have a court injunction. In other words, assuming we are going to lose.

Mr. LYONS. Mr. Smith, if I can just clarify, since obviously the concern is what are we going to do in terms of the short-term timber sale volume? That is my concern too. In fact, I have spent more time in the Northwest than I would have liked, not that I don't enjoy your State, trying to work on the question of the short-term timber supply line.

Now, clearly our primary volume in short-term will come from timber that is already under contract which is being operated. No sales have been stopped. We are proceeding with that.

I have asked for a review of the sales that are under contract to see if there are any sales that clearly do violent harm, if you will, to this proposed plan. That is, have a significant impact on a critical watershed or that. That review is continuing or has been initiated and will continue, but I don't anticipate a significant impact on the timber that is under contract.

Our primary source of timber in the short term is going to be the timber that is currently enjoined, and as Mr. Collier has pointed out, we have a commitment from the plaintiffs to work together to attempt to identify volume that we can go to the court and seek injunctive relief from.

Last week when I was out there we identified 200 million board feet that we think we can move forward with quickly. We are going through a phased process of trying to sit down with the plaintiffs and identify additional volume we can move forward with.

At the same time, I have ordered the Forest Service and BLM to begin the process of preparing new green sales in the American system with option 9.

Mr. ROSE. Thank you, Mr. Lyons, very much.

Mr. Hamburg.

Mr. HAMBURG. Thank you, Mr. Chairman.

I also want to thank the people at the table for their efforts to put together a plan that must be fairly balanced, because I am getting a lot of complaints from both sides, so that usually means that we have to come out to some extent on the middle on this issue. But one of the areas that continues to raise a lot of questions among my constituents are the adaptive management areas, and there is a particularly large one that spans two counties in northern California and that is the Hayfork AMA.

So in the questions that I am going to ask about the AMA, to the extent that you can focus on that one, that is where my primary concern is.

In the forest plan, it talks about the adapted management areas have been geographically located to minimize risk to the overall conservation strategy. I would like to ask, how do you perceive the major risks to take shape? I mean, as Chairman Miller said, we have these areas in which there has not been successful regional planning in the past, and how do you see this taking shape in such a way that we will be able to do the kind of innovative management that you project and that you hope will come about?

Mr. LYONS. Congressman, I would argue that I believe the risks in adaptive management areas may in fact be less than they are in other parts of the forest for this reason: First, the AMA and the management strategies implemented within them are to be consistent with the overall management objectives of the President's forest plan.

Second, the AMA's are areas where we intend to conduct an intensive monitoring and to provide for review and follow up in terms of the kind of experimentation we seek to foster on the ground. We don't have a very effective monitoring system and program in place with regard to the Federal lands we are managing now and we think monitoring is a critical component of the implementation of the AMA strategies.

So that, I hope, will help us to better assess what impacts management may be having and then make corrective changes. That is in fact what adaptive management is, to learn from management experience and then make those changes as we move forward.

Mr. HAMBURG. Jim, what guarantees are we going to have that that monitoring which you admit in the plan, you call it essentially nonexistent throughout the Federal resource management agencies, what is it in this plan that should give us confidence that that monitoring will in fact be done?

I mean, we have some species out there, particularly salmon, where we have a very small margin of error. I believe on the Hayfork AMA there are already nine stocks of salmon that are in danger of extinction. So what should give me confidence, particularly with respect to this AMA, that there is going to be the kind of monitoring done to protect these species? Why don't I get an answer to this. Then I would like to follow up.

Mr. LYONS. The answer is that because these are unique areas, we need to sit down and work up overall management strategies to implement them. We need to ensure that we have the monitoring system in place to do the job.

We have a lot invested, I think, in this kind of approach, in an adaptive management approach, and I think it is critical that we be able to put monitoring in place and demonstrate that we can actually practice what we preach.

Mr. HAMBURG. Jim, I am questioning if whether in areas where we already have species at significant risk, if this is really the place to bring in management practices or ways of looking at managing these areas that are really untried, and I am particularly concerned about salmon.

Let me just ask, what is the viability assessment of salmon in the plan generally?

Mr. LYONS. I will yield to Mr. Sedell on that.

Mr. HAMBURG. Dr. Sedell. What is the viability assessment of salmon?

Mr. SEDELL. Of all the options?

Mr. HAMBURG. Yes. No. Option 9.

Mr. SEDELL. Of option 9?

Mr. HAMBURG. Yes.

Mr. SEDELL. It had an A, B level of 80 or above. It had an A level, a likelihood in which habitat was well distributed throughout the range, around 65.

Mr. HAMBURG. Is that rating based on an understanding that there will be restoration programs carried forth?

Mr. SEDELL. Very much so.

Mr. HAMBURG. What will happen to the fish if Congress doesn't come forward with the funds for those restoration programs?

Mr. SEDELL. It is basically playing roulette with the environment and it is a much longer time period for recovery of habitat for those sensitive stocks.

Mr. HAMBURG. Do you believe that the AMA approach is a good one for helping the stocks that are at risk?

Mr. SEDELL. I assume that it is going to be very much a part of an AMA strategy and would be one of the part and parcels of protecting and restoration.

Mr. HAMBURG. My time is expired.

Thank you, Mr. Chairman.

Mr. ROSE. Mr. Brown of California seeks to make an unanimous-consent request.

Mr. BROWN. Mr. Chairman, thank you.

I just wanted to ask unanimous consent to insert a prepared statement in the record, including some written questions.

Mr. ROSE. Without objection, the prepared statement of Mr. Brown will be placed at the beginning of the hearing.

Mr. BROWN. And welcome to the distinguished witnesses, including Mr. Lyons, perhaps to see him back again.

Mr. ROSE. Thank you, Mr. Brown. Without objection, your request is granted.

Mrs. Unsoeld, I understand Ms. Shepherd wants to yield her time to you. Is that correct?

Ms. SHEPHERD. Yes, it is.

Mr. ROSE. I would be happy to accommodate that arrangement if you would let Mr. LaRocco go next and then you can take it all at one shot.

Mr. LaRocco.

Mrs. UNSOELD. Thank you.

Mr. LAROCCO. Thank you, Mr. Chairman.

Welcome to the panel here. I want to say with regard to the statement that was made by Mr. Collier, in his opening statement, that I think you are the cleanup crew in 1993. I think the administration for 12 years has neglected it and I don't think you are assessing blame. I think it is coming through loud and clear to the people of the Northwest and the people of America what is going on. My colleague from Montana who was here earlier, is working on a Montana wilderness bill that is not truly unlike what was vetoed by President Reagan back in 1988, and so we have had so much turmoil out in the Rocky Mountain region due to the fact that we just haven't gotten on with managing under the laws and doing the appropriate things.

The chairman of the board of Boise Cascade said the day before your plan came out, option 9, that 200,000 jobs would be lost.

Is this anywhere in the ballpark and how would you respond to that?

Mr. GREBER. You said that there was a study that said 200,000 jobs would be lost?

Mr. LAROCCO. I believe it was John Ferry from Boise Cascade who made the statement that 200,000 jobs would be lost.

Mr. GREBER. I have not seen that study so I can't——

Mr. LAROCCO. He just made the statement.

Mr. GREBER. I cannot say what he was using as his comparison for what those 200,000 jobs were lost from.

Mr. LAROCCO. Labor and industry are saying that 85,000 jobs are going to be lost. Does that jibe with your projections?

Mr. GREBER. You could reconstruct that scenario. When you talk about job losses, I have to define what are you losing jobs from, and I can see very logically scenarios that one could design that would generate an 85,000-job-loss figure that would have the exact same employment forecasts that are in our numbers.

Mr. LAROCCO. Well, that question is being asked—those statements and figures are being used in my district in north Idaho. There are petitions circulating around there against option 9 right now based on the 85,000 job loss figure. I think if the administration disagrees with those, I think we should look to see how you feel those numbers are not accurate.

Mr. COLLIER. Congressman, if I could add a little bit to that. There are two things you have to look at when you start talking about job loss numbers. The first is the base, what are they comparing it to, and then the second is whether they are including indirect jobs or only direct jobs.

When you look at the 85,000 and you use a base farther back during the historic timber levels, and you include indirect jobs, I don't know whether they are close or they are far off; I haven't analyzed it that carefully, but when we look at a 1992 baseline and a direct job loss only, we are very confident in our 6,000 estimate, and we think it is a solid estimate.

Now, I don't want to take issue with whether or not you ought to count indirect jobs. We were looking at what is it in terms of jobs we want to try to have an economic package that addresses, and that is why we came out with the 6,000.

We believed if we replaced those 6,000, we would also be replacing the indirect jobs that go with them. So that is why we focused on direct job loss and we looked at the 1992 base and that is how we came out with our 6,000. I would imagine that is the difference between our number and any other numbers. If you ask those two questions, you will get the answer.

Mr. LaRocco. In other words, perhaps how big the multiplier effect is and how that reverberates around the region?

Mr. COLLIER. And what the baseline is that you are comparing to.

Mr. GREBER. For clarification, if you look at our numbers in the region, in the region's timber industry, 1988 there were 152,000 jobs. Under option 9, that drops to 119,800. Now, you could say that in that period of time there were 32,200 jobs lost from 1988 to option 9, and then if you applied an indirect and induced multiplier of 1.12, you are up to 70,000 jobs.

So that is a selection of 1988 as a baseline. If you choose 1992 as a baseline, you are starting with the 125,400 jobs and dropping down to 119,800 jobs.

Mr. LaRocco. Thank you.

I just want to make the quick comment that I have heard from people out in the Northwest that perhaps the administration has dealt with this problem with a great deal of intensity and now that there tends to be a reduction in the amount of work at the staff level that is being dedicated to this problem, and I would just hope we stay with the same intensity to resolve this.

Thank you, Mr. Chairman.

Mr. ROSE. Thank you very much.

Mr. Lewis.

Mr. LEWIS. Mr. Chairman, I yield 5 minutes to Mr. Pombo of California.

Mr. POMBO. Thank you.

Just to clarify something you just said that maybe I misunderstood you. Did you say that you were using 1992 as your baseline for job loss?

Mr. GREBER. I never used a baseline for job losses. I reported historic employment levels and a future projection for exactly the reason that we are talking about. You can play a lot of games with selection of a base for expressing job losses.

So there is not a baseline established within the FEMAT report.

Mr. POMBO. Sorry. I thought I heard you say 1992.

Mr. GREBER. I said if you selected 1992 as a base, and before that I said if you selected 1988 as a base to demonstrate selection of a base can skew the numbers quite a bit.

Mr. COLLIER. Congressman, to help you with that, if I might, he is referring to the scientific report that we received. As we translated his calculation in job loss numbers, which is an addition and subtraction process, we used 1992 as our baseline.

Mr. POMBO. So you did use——

Mr. COLLIER. We did. He didn't. We used his numbers to make that calculation.

Mr. POMBO. But in 1992, the—I guess what you guys are trying to do is get away from the shutdown of the industry that happened in 1992, and if you are using that as your baseline, you are showing the basic shutdown of the industry in 1992 and we are only going to lose 6,000 from there?

Mr. COLLIER. Congressman, 2 things. One is there was still a lot of timber in the pipeline in 1992 and the second thing is, we weren't trying to hide what we were doing a bit.

If you want to go back and look 2 years further at 1990, I believe we calculated that number and it is in the report also.

Mr. POMBO. I have another question that has to do with the takings analysis that was done. I am sure you have done a takings analysis under this, and what is your estimated cost of the takings of private property under this option?

Mr. COLLIER. What takings are you referring to?

Mr. POMBO. Under the fifth amendment, takings of private property and the further restrictions on their ability to use their private property.

Mr. COLLIER. We have not concluded that we have a fifth amendment takings problem at this point, Congressman.

Mr. POMBO. So are you telling me that there is not going to be any loss of value to the private property, its effect in this area?

Mr. COLLIER. Congressman, I hope the result of this plan is that we free up a lot of private lands that is currently under restrictions, not that we are adding restrictions to other private land.

Mr. POMBO. Thank you.

I would like to yield the balance of my time to Mr. Herger.

Mr. ROSE. Without objection, so ordered.

Mr. HERGER. Thank you very much, Mr. Pombo.

Just continuing this, Mr. Collier, because this is certainly an area—it is tragic enough of all the mills and the real people, real families, third, fourth, and fifth generations working in the woods that are out of work, without trifling with numbers, if you will.

Now, you have mentioned we are using 1992 as a baseline. I am sure—in my district, probably in 1992, because of what had happened in 1990 and because we were looking for a balanced program that would help to some degree rectify what had happened in 1990, we probably had about 20 mills close at that time.

So I can assure you, the citizens in my district would look with strong distaste at what would appear to be a gross misrepresentation of how tragic these numbers really are and not looking at indirect jobs, all the service stations and the restaurants and everything else that are used because of what you would say would be 9,000 or 6,000, which we feel is dramatically underestimated, but again—but that is a statement, I suppose.

Just getting back again to the great concern in our area, Mr. Lyons, is the health of our forests; 400,000 acres of timber burned in 1987 were subject to that. Again, I would like to request of you, Mr. Lyons, that you would request of the administration to reconsider the unique characteristics and particularly fire characteristics of northern California in another study.

Mr. ROSE. I thank the gentleman. Your time has expired and——

Mr. HERGER. Is that not a yes, you would request?

Mr. LYONS. Let me answer your original question, Mr. Herger.

Mr. ROSE. Mr. Lyons, please be brief. We are out of time.

Mr. HERGER. I saw you shaking your head.

Mr. LYONS. I want to make it clear that we did consider those characteristics in preparing the original study. We will continue to look at those issues.

Mr. ROSE. Thank you.

Mrs. Unsoeld is recognized for 10 minutes.

Mrs. UNSOELD. Thank you, Mr. Chairman.

Will the clock run through two cycles or one extended?

Mr. ROSE. We will do it twice.

Mrs. UNSOELD. Thank you.

First, Mr. Chairman, I would like to clarify something that I think may have been misunderstood. The payment to the counties, the ALO counties is a part of the President's economic package, is it not?

Mr. LYONS. It is.

Mrs. UNSOELD. So it is not an add-on. Thank you.

And second, our constituents do want us to cut waste, and probably this week we are going to hear a crescendo of rhetoric demanding a cut in waste before we have any additional taxes. I would like to caution my colleagues that we are probably all guilty of being too casual in our demands for additional studies and reconsideration of administrative agencies, and we should look with a real jaundiced eye as to our motives and the worth of those requests that we make before we so casually drop them into the record.

Third, Mr. Chairman, I would like to ask for clarification. Did I hear somebody say that you have gotten the plaintiffs to join you in going to the court?

Mr. COLLIER. I thought maybe you had missed that point. We have been working on this since we announced the plan. We don't have all the i's dotted and t's crossed, but I do have a letter from them that I received this morning that says they are committed to working with us.

All we have to do now is identify the specific sales. We will be going to the courts promptly with a joint motion asking Judge Dwyer to allow certain sales to proceed, notwithstanding the injunction.

Now, this is part of our effort to get timber into those communities as quickly as we can.

Mrs./UNSOELD. Mr. Chairman, that really is an astounding announcement, and I think that you deserve a great deal of credit and praise for having brought us to this stage.

I would like some discussion of the scientific panels and how you anticipate that is going to function in regard to two areas. One, the probability of survival of the range of species and, two, in conjunction with how the adaptive management areas would function.

Mr. LYONS. With regard to how the adaptive management areas would function, Congresswoman, those areas were identified as a means of trying to achieve two things.

First of all, I think to demonstrate that we have the capability to manage resources to deal with the resource problems we face out there and achieve the overall objectives set in the forest plan.

I think, second of all and most importantly is to demonstrate that adaptive management works. We are creating a situation, we hope, that is a laboratory to try different silvicultural techniques to understand the relationship between management and impacts on both timber and nontimber resources, and also to experiment with different ways of involving the public more directly in making management choices and management decisions.

Mrs. UNSOELD. And how about in how you assess the probability of survival of the range of species so that we are not dealing with crises by crises? How does the scientific panel function in that regard or how do you anticipate that it will?

Mr. J. THOMAS. We developed a means of looking at that broad spectrum of species by taking expert panels, 14 panels of experts and asking them essentially in the question that you asked—we gave them four likely outcomes based on the regulations and in the National Forest Management Act; are viable populations well distributed? Are viable populations not well distributed? Are viable populations—C well distributed, but in pockets or refugia not well distributed; and I asked them to assess the situation in terms of habitat for species across that entire spectrum.

Now, while I would not, with the exception of a few species, bet the farm on the assessment of those individually, collectively they add up to a rather definitive picture of how one might best go about indeed preserving that entire ecosystem and the parts thereof, and there are risk assessments associated and they are very different between options.

Mrs. UNSOELD. In the adaptive management areas, the scientific panel has an overall check of what is being done. But isn't one of the values of how those areas would be managed, is it against the communities' invested interest in the outcome of sustainable management, sustainable use of the resource?

Mr. LYONS. That is precisely the case, Mrs. Unsold. These areas weren't placed at random across the landscape. They were placed in areas where communities had either already made an investment in attempting to affect management and management direction, or in areas where communities certainly are impacted by changes in Federal timber supply.

And we seek an opportunity in establishing these adaptive management areas to foster a greater and closer cooperation with the communities so as to allow them to help determine what future management direction will be to maintain sustainable production of timber and other resources those communities might depend on.

One of the concepts we are exploring, in fact, is trying to keep the timber supply from a given adaptive management area within that local region to benefit local mills and other sectors of the industry that might use wood products.

We are trying some innovative approaches to management to hopefully move things along and reduce some of the conflict and confrontation that we see currently causing the problems in the region.

Mrs. UNSOELD. In Washington State, two-thirds of our timber base is privately owned or at least non-Federal, State, and private, but we can't get very far with an ecosystem management or watershed restoration protection without involving the private landowners in managing the landscape.

How are we going to get cooperation and involvement of private timber landowners in the ecosystem management approach?

Mr. LYONS. I think we have seen, Congresswoman, that everyone in the region has a vested interest in working together to try and provide the raw material needs for the industry as well as to provide for protection of environmental values that are also important to the region.

Again, referring to the adaptive management areas, several were designed in mixed ownerships to try and foster that cooperation and coordination. I hope it is reflective of the fact that I think perhaps this crisis has brought people to realize that it is important that we do work together to try and move forward to manage our way out of this crisis as opposed to allow the status quo to remain.

Mrs. UNSOELD. I am trying to give you an opportunity to give the value to the private landowners in your working on the 4(d) rule.

Mr. LYONS. I thought you were headed in that direction, but I thought I would beat the dead horse on adaptive management areas first.

Let me allow Tom Collier, whose staff has been involved in developing the 4(d) rule, give you an update on where that stands.

Mr. COLLIER. The 4(d) rule looks at how we can lift the owl restrictions that have been on a lot of the land. And as we have looked at that, we have looked at what other restrictions might need to be in place for the owl.

There is some question as to whether some of that we could locate along riparian zones and kind of get a two-fer out of the rule. We would provide some habitat for owls and, at the same time, we would provide some additional watershed protection, with a final benefit for the private landowner of when the at-risk fish stocks that may be listed are listed. They are already ahead of the game in terms of how they are going to manage their lands.

We are not sure how far we will be able to take that process within the context of 4(d). Because within the context of 4(d), we are limited to the confines of species and we will stay within the confines of that portion of the statute.

But another option we are looking at are using habitat conservation plans and coming up with some models that we could make available to industry and see if we could not do something along the lines of what we did for the red-cockaded woodpecker down in the Southeast that would provide existing protection and also be looking forward in the future as to what we see coming down the pike, so that a particularly cooperative landowner would get some future benefits out of agreeing to that type of HCP.

Mr. ROSE. One minute left.

Mrs. UNSOELD. On the total?

Mr. ROSE. Is that the first 5 minutes or the whole?

Mrs. UNSOELD. The whole.

I will make a statement, because I believe that what you all sitting at this table, and some of your colleagues, have undergone in the way of abuse from us in Government in what we have requested you to do and the kind of attack you have often been under, I want to express a thank you for what you have done, what you are still doing for us, and to say that the proof of the value of what you have done, if in nothing else—and I think there is a lot that we can point to—but in your being able to take to the judge, to the court, a request for the injunctions to be lifted with which we have been living so long.

So my congratulations to all of you and my thanks from the Northwest for what you have done.

Mr. ROSE. Thank you very much. The gentlelady's time has expired. Mr. Lewis.

Mr. LEWIS. I recognize Mr. Doolittle from California for 5 minutes.

Mr. DOOLITTLE. I yield my time to Mr. Smith of Oregon.

Mr. SMITH of Oregon. I thank the gentleman very much for yielding.

Dr. Greber, we are all confused about the relative numbers of jobs lost, and let me get at it another way, if I can. The administration says that there will be 6,000 direct jobs lost. You offered at the timber conference a recommendation, I believe, and you identified job loss.

What was the number of jobs lost that you recommended in your presentation to the conference in Portland? Let me ask it this way: What was your multiplier, Dr. Greber.

Mr. GREBER. The multiplier I was using was roughly 14 jobs per million board foot.

Mr. SMITH of Oregon. So at 14 jobs per million board feet, and we are going to lose 4 billion, that is above 55,000 jobs lost?

Mr. GREBER. That is with indirect and induced effects, correct.

Mr. SMITH of Oregon. So you have told the conference that the multiplier, in your opinion, ought to be 14; and so all we have to do—that is indirect and direct jobs lost?

Mr. GREBER. Correct.

Mr. SMITH of Oregon. So all we have to do is determine the loss and multiply that. Obviously, the loss of sale quality is down to 1.2 billion from historically, roughly, 5 billion in that region?

Mr. GREBER. Correct.

Mr. SMITH of Oregon. Thank you.

Mr. GREBER. I will say, Congressman, that we actually increased the multiplier within the course of this study. That was some of the growth in value-added manufacturing and some of the other sectors in the Pacific Northwest economy and the industry folks seen on the raw material recovery. We actually increased our multiplier somewhat from that study.

So I can't recall the exact number, but it is higher than the multiplier that was used in the forest conference.

Mr. SMITH of Oregon. It is higher than 14?

Mr. GREBER. Yes, sir.

Mr. SMITH of Oregon. Is it 20?

Mr. GREBER. It is not that high. I can reconstruct it for you, if you would like.

Mr. SMITH of Oregon. Please, if you just give me a number, I can multiply by 4 billion.

Mr. GREBER. It actually comes out to be—excuse me. 16.5.

Mr. SMITH of Oregon. 16.5 times 4 billion is how much? Somebody?

Mr. DOOLITTLE. 66,000.

Mr. SMITH of Oregon. 66,000, roughly.

Mr. GREBER. Correct.

Mr. SMITH of Oregon. Thank you.

Dr. Thomas, I want to read from a letter I received from the Fish and Wildlife Service in Portland signed by Marvin Plenert, whom you know—I hope this does not cost him his job—about the impact upon the timber sale in the Ashland watershed on spotted owls.

"The result was that owls seemed to cope with the light touch of activities very easily, even while on the nest, while nearly 10 million board feet of timber were removed. We do not believe that this activity has created any threat to the survival or recovery of the owl. Indeed, we believe the forest habitat has been improved by creating a multistoried canopy with the remaining debris for forage habitat.

Do you agree with that?

Mr. J. THOMAS. I have no idea what he is talking about.

Mr. SMITH of Oregon. He is talking about harvesting timber in spotted owl areas. They took 10 million board feet out of the Ashland watershed.

Mr. J. THOMAS. Congressman, I am not familiar with that.

Mr. SMITH of Oregon. Do you agree you can harvest timber in spotted owl habitat?

Mr. J. THOMAS. Would I agree with what?

Mr. SMITH of Oregon. That you can harvest timber near spotted owl nests and not injure spotted owls?

Mr. J. THOMAS. Depends on how it is done.

Mr. SMITH of Oregon. Depends on how it is done. It can be done?

Mr. J. THOMAS. Depends on the circumstances.

Mr. SMITH of Oregon. It can be done?

Mr. J. THOMAS. Again, it depends on the circumstances.

Mr. SMITH of Oregon. Well, it is either one way or the other. You just told us it can be done.

Mr. J. THOMAS. I just told you it depends on the circumstances.

Mr. SMITH of Oregon. If the circumstances——

Mr. J. THOMAS. I won't give you a yes or no answer because it is not a yes or no question. It depends on the circumstances.

Mr. SMITH of Oregon. The point is, here is a biologist of some renown saying it did not injure the spotted owl by harvesting timber. What are you saying?

Mr. J. THOMAS. I have not read the letter and it is unfair to ask me a question on something that I am not familiar with—the document you are looking at. I would assume it means there was a case where they harvested, a situation, and the owl remained. How much they took, how they did it, what the circumstances were, I do not know. It is very difficult for me——

Mr. SMITH of Oregon. Your promise is to set aside 9 million acres in alternate nine. Nine million acres that cannot be touched. That is your alternative?

Mr. J. THOMAS. That is not so.

Mr. SMITH of Oregon. That is alternative nine.

Mr. J. THOMAS. No, it is not.

Mr. SMITH of Oregon. What is alternative nine?

Mr. J. THOMAS. Alternate set-asides—I don't know the exact number, but it allows for thinning both of young stands up to age 80, both of plantations and of naturally regenerated stands. It calls for intervention under an appropriate plan on the east side and the Klamath Province to deal with fire situations in danger. It is not a total reserve.

Mr. VENTO [assuming chair]. The time of the gentleman has expired. Mr. Farr is recognized for 5 minutes.

Mr. FARR. Thank you very much, Mr. Chairman. I would like to compliment you and your cochairs on calling this joint hearing. It is very informative. And I would also like to compliment the panel on rising to the challenge that they had to face. I think they have done a remarkable job faced with very tough circumstances.

I have two questions that I am interested in. Both come from my own personal background of, one, representing a county that is the smallest county in California, Santa Cruz County, but is a major contributor to timber harvesting, both on private and State lands; and, two, working as a hotshot crew in the U.S. Forest Service on a firefighting crew during college.

The issue I am interested in affects the State of California. Essentially, it is the interface. California has been faced with a drought. The drought has caused a lot of beetle infection. The beetle infection and the drought have caused scores of dead trees, leading to a large fuel load increase.

The State of California, department of forestry, has the responsibility for fires and interfaces with the private sector, private lands, and particularly has a difficult mission ahead of them in the checkerboard ownership in northern California with the U.S. Forest Service plans outlined today.

My question is: Because of the legal duty issue that the State has to face in the agreements they have developed, will there be any compensation for the State of California beyond the community assistance that you outlined for the owl communities or owl counties, to help the State in their fire prevention management?

Mr. LYONS. Well, Congressman, I don't know if I can answer that question immediately. I am not sure what the specific resource needs would be and how implementation of this plan might affect the fire responsibilities of the State. It is certainly something we can look at to determine if additional resources are needed.

Mr. FARR. I believe it also greatly affects the salvage sale for dead fuel policy when it is worked out. Do you have a timeframe when you will have the policy regulations determined?

Mr. LYONS. I can't tell you that offhand, but I can find out for you, Congressman, and send it to your office.

Mr. FARR. Thank you.

And last, with the Federal short supply driving up the cost of timber, it is going to put more pressure on private lands, as you have indicated, and as you have wanted to happen, and result in more pressure on State lands. Those are going to require, under our timber harvest management plan in California, greatly increased cost to the State department of forestry to process those timber harvest plans on both State and private lands.

Is there going to be any compensation or ability to help the State address those increased pressures?

Mr. LYONS. Well, as you know, Congressman, I think we have a good working relationship with Terry Gordon and the State people, and we will continue to work with them to see if there is need to identify additional resources or to make changes in management priorities in the region to help facilitate the implementation of this plan.

If it causes any additional impact on California's forest program, we will attempt to work with them to see if we can work things out.

Mr. FARR. I would appreciate that. We will submit to you some cost estimates from the State of California and we would hope you could address those.

Mr. LYONS. I had a feeling you might have those.

Mr. FARR. Thank you. I will yield the remainder of my time.

Mr. VENTO. Will the gentleman yield?

Mr. FARR. Yes, sir.

Mr. VENTO. There has been some discussion about the loss of jobs on private lands, but you used a figure of 9.6 or 9.8 in the executive summary of the document in terms of the mid-1980's, and point out that the projections are actually that they would become and are less today and they would be less in the future; is that correct?

Don't you use that in the executive summary, Mr. Collier?

Mr. COLLIER. I am not familiar with that number, Congressman. I am sorry.

Mr. VENTO. I wanted to point it out, because I thought that the summary says that the Washington outlook and—well, that is a different statement. But I think in that executive summary it points out the number of job losses even in the private sector lands are less than in terms of what your projections are from what they are today.

In fact, is there any assessment here of the fishery jobs? We are talking, obviously, about jobs.

Mr. Greber.

Mr. GREBER. We did an assessment of the current level of employment in commercial fisheries in Washington and Oregon. We did not do any forecasts of how these plans might alter that employment level, but we did assess current employment levels.

Mr. VENTO. Well, the point is, if one were to assume that they were to remain constant as opposed to change, since there is a relationship apparently between the—of course, there is all sorts of controversy about this, and we can probably get into that, too—but that the timber harvest in an excessive way has had an adverse effect on the fisheries, and that if you assume this particular trade-off, obviously, it would or should be considered a credit for probably following this ecosystem management that you are putting out; isn't that correct, Dr. Greber?

Mr. GREBER. In the long run, you should see some gains in the commercial fisheries and the recreation fisheries related industries.

Mr. VENTO. Mr. Farr's time has expired.

Mr. Volkmer.

Mr. VOLKMER. I personally want to apologize to Jerry Franklin for not including him in the "Gang of Four" at the table. The reporter was between me and I didn't notice you there. I want to say thank you, too.

But I have several things. First, I want to make a little statement and maybe clarify some things.

In defense of the panel and Mr. Lyons and this administration, who are, in my opinion, attempting for the first time to try to resolve the issue in the Northwest, I can well remember—Jim, I am not going to ask you, to put you on the spot, to verify what I am going to say; but as one who was working right with me at the time, and the others at the panel, you know back in 1990 there was a little court order that required the then-administration to come up with a proposal.

And those of us who were, as chairman then of the Forestry Subcommittee, and those of us working on it along with Interior and others, anxiously awaited for that proposal. It was supposed to come out in September. And in September, we got a three-page news release. And that is all that I ever saw that was ever done by the previous administration in an attempt to solve the problem in the Northwest. And we anxiously awaited through 1990, 1991, and 1992 without any efforts.

I want to commend you for your effort that is being made, because I look upon it, if we just sat back and took the same approach that was taken before, and you had done that, where would we be as far as sales for next year? We are talking about, are we not, on the west side, we are talking about region 6 on the west side; northern California, region 5; right? Not talking the east side; is that right?

Mr. LYONS. That is correct.

Mr. VOLKMER. Where would we be as far as proposed sales next year without any activity whatsoever?

Mr. LYONS. Well, we would simply be able to offer those sales under contract that have already passed section 7 consultation.

Mr. VOLKMER. Right.

Mr. LYONS. We would still face the injunctions currently in place and, frankly, that has precluded the ability to prepare any new sales, so the pipeline has virtually run dry.

Mr. VOLKMER. So the existing sales—and even if you attempted sales and some of those were approved through fish and wildlife, et cetera, if that was done, you would still undoubtedly run into appeals to those sales; correct?

Mr. LYONS. Correct.

Mr. VOLKMER. So in a couple of years, we would have nothing in the pipeline and it is all dried up.

Mr. LYONS. That is right.

Mr. VOLKMER. So I think everybody should recognize that.

The other thing I think people should recognize, and as one who worked strenuously back on H.R. 4899 and saw that one, too, was a compromise and it was an attempt to again arrive at a solution—and the gentleman from California, Mr. Hamburg, you said this must be a good proposal. Well, those of us who have been through this for years recognize that when you have something that you feel is actually accomplishing a purpose out there, you will find that there are both sides that are going to condemn you for doing it and tell you that it is no good.

And that is why I want to commend this administration for knowing that, knowing that you are getting into that field and attempting to arrive at a solution anyway.

And for those of you—I guess especially we don't have many freshmen left around. Mr. Hamburg is still here, and there are a couple on this side. This is, again, just that part of the owl forests out there. We still have the problem with the east side; right, Jack?

Mr. J. THOMAS. Yes.

Mr. VOLKMER. We have that coming at us. We have the Sierras in California; is that right, Jim?

Mr. LYONS. That is correct.

Mr. VOLKMER. And we have the others, the Northern Rockies, Central Rockies, and other areas too that still have to be addressed. And, Jack, Jerry, I would like to ask you all a question here.

As one who has listened to you and learned from you over the years about a different approach to managing a forest, we don't know, do we, everything we need to know yet about an ecological management of our national forest or any forest yet?

Mr. FRANKLIN. That is very correct, Mr. Congressman. We do not know, and I think it is really important that we recognize that as we go about implementing this or any other plan; that we have to learn as we go, and that, in effect, we are conducting experiments with every decision we make.

Now, the implication of that is that we really need to begin to monitor for the first time so that we can assess how well we are doing with our experiments.

Mr. VOLKMER. And so you would foresee that as we develop the plan, and if it is approved by the court and as it goes on, there are going to be changes made, necessarily, in that plan; is that correct?

Mr. FRANKLIN. That is certainly correct. We certainly will.

Mr. VOLKMER. And we will have to do additional research into various areas in order to learn more than what we know now; is that correct, also?

Mr. FRANKLIN. That is absolutely correct, Mr. Congressman.

Mr. VOLKMER. Now, I hope that everyone recognizes that and that what is being proposed here is not just an end but a beginning.

And I want to again commend those within the administration for daring to tread this road because you are not going to get a lot of bouquets as you go down the road.

Thank you, Mr. Chairman.

Mr. VENTO. Thank you, Harold, for keeping within the time.

Mr. Lewis, do you want to recognize——

Mr. LEWIS. Mr. Kingston of Georgia for 5 minutes.

Mr. KINGSTON. Thank you, Mr. Lewis. I have one question in the spirit of just making a point. We kind of, as usual, in the current administration, I would say, open statements always blaming everything on the last 12 years and the failed policies of the past. Gridlock. And certainly your testimony, particularly Mr. Collier's, was full of that, at least with the first five pages.

Would you blame the previous administration for not typing on both sides of the paper today? I ask that because I noticed Mr. Lyons was environmentally correct in his testimony. Shame on the rest of you guys. And I hope the next time that the committee and the Secretary send folks down here, they do use both sides of the paper in the name of environmental protection and saving the Earth.

I am being a little bit sarcastic only because I still feel the sting of the first five pages of your testimony, and I really and truly hope that we get to the point in this administration where everything is not just, OK, let's start out being Democrats and Republicans.

I am a new member. I represent a district that is not interested in partisan politics and that is all this is: Well, the failed policies of the past. I mean, give us a break. Let's start off with a little integrity. These issues are way too important to start out with the usual partisan diatribes. And that might be Washington, I am not trying to blame it on you guys. Maybe that is everything, because it certainly seems to be the case, but this almost sounds like a budget hearing here, which is partisan.

The Ag Committee, which I am a member of, Merchant Marine and Fisheries Committee I am also a member of, they are generally bipartisan committees. You have environmentalists and less than environmentalists on there, but I just hope that we can get there. And I am not asking for a response, I am just making that statement.

I am speaking from a new Member's perspective and I want to yield my time.

Mr. COLLIER. May I make a short response?

Mr. KINGSTON. It would only be fair, wouldn't it?

Mr. COLLIER. Point well made. I look forward to working with you as we move ahead.

Mr. KINGSTON. Thank you.

Mr. Taylor, yield my time.

Mr. VENTO. Gentleman yields back his time.

Mr. LEWIS. He wants to yield his time, Mr. Chairman, to Mr. Taylor of North Carolina.

Mr. VENTO. Without objection.

Mr. TAYLOR of North Carolina. Thank you, Mr. Chairman.

In the brief time I have, I would like to sort of sum up what I have heard. I know there is a jobs program. About $1.2 billion in economic assistance going in for a jobs program.

I look at the 1978 program in the Redwoods National Forest, where there was a very lucrative jobs program brought to the area, and of the 3,500 people that received benefits of that program, less than 10 percent retained a job after the first several months.

And so to show that there is very little hope of economic success in the Pacific Northwest by pumping in additional dollars when you take out this basic infrastructure, I would like to look at where we are compared to where we have been brought, what we have actually done with this plan that is ratcheted down to $1.2 billion.

That is not taking into consideration the infrastructure necessary to maintain harvest in those areas and not taking into consideration survival of special infrastructure that will keep environmentalists off of you while you are trying to harvest that. This plan is, unfortunately, based upon the same laws that were created by myth and poor science, and the same pressures for court actions and other actions are going to be there. So I doubt we will ever harvest the $1.2 billion.

There are some 5,000 endangered species and/or candidates coming up. So what I am saying is, I would hope this administration would not just rearrange the deck chairs on the Titanic but we would pull back and take a real look at how we got to this place. Otherwise, there are other parts of the country, as Mr. Volkmer mentioned a while ago in the west Sierra, areas in the South, Southeast, that will face these same problems and we will find that the same goofy reasons we got to this point today will be there. And we will forget about the 80,000 jobs that are being lost in the Pacific Northwest, because there will be so many being lost all over the country that those will be minuscule.

We need to go back and reassess those laws that brought us to this point, Mr. Chairman.

Mr. VENTO. The gentleman has yielded back the balance of his time, or do you want a response from the witness?

Mr. TAYLOR of North Carolina. Seeing the light, I thought that was my time, but I will yield such of it as was left.

Mr. VENTO. The gentleman yields back his time. All have been recognized, so we will start a second round of questions and the chairman will take 5 minutes.

I would just comment to my friend from North Carolina that there have been 27,000 resolutions under the Endangered Species Act. A few of them get a lot more attention, including, of course, the spotted owl. One way to deal with this, of course, is the way that Secretary Babbitt has taken the lead in dealing with a number of different problems, not the least of which, of course, is this matter we are dealing with here, the 1,400 different species.

One question on that point. In looking at the options, it looks like the plan does pretty well by vertebrates, but as far as invertebrates and nonvascular plants, as well as some vascular plants, the likelihood of maintaining stable populations does not fare as well.

Can you explain that, Dr. Thomas?

Mr. J. THOMAS. Yes, sir, I think fairly simple. The panels that evaluated that feel it is strongly related to the amount of area in reserve, and also strongly related to what can happen inside of a reserve; whether you can cut it or not cut it, salvage it or not salvage it; what would happen in the matrix between reserves, depending on how much downed logs or other inherited factors from previous stands are left by particular management option. It also depends on the extent of the riparian zone protection.

In combination, those things add up to make, I think, in the minds of the panels, made the difference.

Mr. VENTO. I think it is important to note that there are some risks inherent in the plan. Obviously, one of them is the changes in terms of policy with reserves as they affect them.

Do we envision in the use of this that there is salvage and other types of disease harvest in reserves which is discussed. Of course, we don't have all the details on that, or at least I don't, but what does that mean; that we will have new roads put into reserves? Is that anticipated or not?

Mr. J. THOMAS. The rule for salvage in a reserve or for thinning in a reserve is that it would benefit, either be neutral to or benefit the long-term objective of the reserve, which is late-successional or old-growth forest condition. Obviously, there would be road construction that would go along with those thinnings in order to retrieve the material or with salvage.

However, the extent of that varies very much from situation to situation. Keep in mind that these are not roadless areas. In many cases, perhaps 40 percent of the area is presently in late-successional or old-growth forest condition, and many of the areas are quite extensively roaded.

Mr. VENTO. I was concerned, of course, about new roads to do salvage or disease. The other issue is thinning, which you brought up, and there is some—really, this thinning idea is more in the experimental stage, is it not, Dr. Thomas, to know what the effect will be?

If you want to yield to others, Dr. Franklin or others, I would be glad to hear from them.

Mr. J. THOMAS. I will take a try and then perhaps Dr. Franklin can jump in.

There is not unanimous agreement among experts about what the effects of thinning would be, and is divided into two cases. One is the thinning of plantations, which are trees that have been harvested and then replanted. There is less concern about thinning in plantations in order to produce faster growing, wider spaced trees and a multiple canopy.

The other consideration is the thinning and naturally regenerated stands that come back from fire or blow-down. There really is not enough empirical evidence to judge emphatically what the result would be.

Mr. VENTO. I will leave it at that.

And I have another question for Dr. Franklin, but I don't want to miss the opportunity to commend the Departments of the Interior and Agriculture, Mr. Collier and Mr. Lyons, for their efforts in terms of trying to work with the conservation groups to get back to court.

I think you are right. I think that Congresswoman Unsoeld underlined a very important point that was made that most of us glossed over, and I think it is enormously important if we are to resolve this, to get it out of the courts and back into the hands of land managers, and that is what is happening here.

And whatever intentions were of past administrations, we can go over that a long time. They gambled and they lost, and they lost big time. And the truth is, I think now that we have to come back and visit this, the options are fewer than they otherwise would be. But certainly getting those folks back into the idea of lifting the injunctions is important.

I would point out, I know Dr. Franklin, you have been doing some work in Native American lands and reservations in terms of timber harvest. We had some statements here earlier about that. Do you generally agree what the problems are, the dimensions of the problems in terms of meeting those targets, in terms of gaining greater wood fiber from these areas?

Mr. FRANKLIN. My impression, after being a part of the Indian Forest management assessment team, is that the same kind of conflicts that exist on our national forests also exist on most reservations, and that often, the tribes do not have a clear consensus on what they want to do.

Mr. VENTO. But improving that management will yield or will make possible to harvest, if in fact it is their policy decision to move ahead and there is a capacity to harvest some amount of fiber that would offset the losses from other areas due to this plan?

Mr. FRANKLIN. Some reservations appear to have additional capacity if the funding were available to do additional silvicultural treatments and harvest.

Mr. VENTO. My time has expired as you can see. I guess the question goes to Mr. Taylor. Five minutes.

Mr. TAYLOR of North Carolina. Thank you, Mr. Chairman.

I understand in the $1.2 billion in economic assistance, about half of it, $600 million, is going to reforestation, and I will ask this of Mr. Lyons or anyone else that cares to answer.

Has there not been reforestation funds available to the Forest Service in the past? Why this necessity for $600 million for reforestation?

Mr. LYONS. I am not sure quite how to answer that immediately, Congressman. There have been reforestation funds in the past and, of course, some of the reforestation occurs under K–V funds.

I will have to look into that.

Mr. TAYLOR of North Carolina. Could you tell me, is any of it going to private landowners or is it all federally reforested?

Mr. LYONS. The funds I think that you are referring to would be for reforestation on National Forest System lands. Of course, we have several programs that you are aware of, the forestry incentive program, stewardship incentive programs to provide assistance to private lands.

Mr. TAYLOR of North Carolina. You can give me a more specific answer, when you have a chance to look.

I would ask about the 1.2 billion board feet annually in the spotted owl forest that is being set aside, how much of that do we envision to come from private lands? Is all of that coming from Federal lands?

Mr. LYONS. That is an estimate of annual sustained yield harvest from the owl forests, which are all Federal lands, Forest Service and BLM lands, on the west side of the Cascades in Oregon, Washington, and northern California. Actually, I guess the private lands in the region accounts for two-thirds of the total harvest in the region. So substantially more harvest will come from private lands.

Mr. TAYLOR of North Carolina. The administration had talked about getting timber to the timber-starved mills as quickly as possible. What is now flowing and what do you envision flowing to that region as far as the mills of that region are concerned in the next several months?

Is there any sort of schedule you can give me?

Mr. LYONS. Again, Congressman, sales under contract are proceeding with the agreement we have reached with the plaintiffs to pursue an attempt to lift or achieve partial lifting of the injunction.

Looking at patches of sales, those sales with minimal rework will then be available to move forward and move to the mills.

That is where our short-term volume will come from, sales under contract and those sales we can get injunctive relief from.

As we move forward in preparing new green sales, one of the things where we need to look at, and one of the things I have discussed with some of the interagency people, is identifying those mills in communities of greatest need and trying to target our resources and our efforts to prepare as a priority additional volume in those parts of the country.

Mr. TAYLOR of North Carolina. I understand that some of the reforestation will take place in roads and other areas that have been kept open for harvesting.

Do you intend in those reforested areas to ever harvest any of that timber that is being reforested with the $600 million?

Mr. LYONS. Again, I am not quite certain how those points are intended to be expended, so I need to look into that. We certainly will be reforesting all those areas that have been cut over.

I know we will reforest areas where we have had reforestation failures in the past. I can't assure that in all instances all those trees will be part of the future timber base. But certainly we have an obligation to curb soil erosion and other concerns, so we need to make sure those areas are reforested.

Mr. TAYLOR of North Carolina. Thank you.

Could someone address the question of job creation? I mentioned earlier, not knowing we would have a second chance, that I was somewhat concerned about the 1978 job plans, that less than 10 percent of the people who received benefits for job training and so forth stayed there after a few months at a job.

Are you familiar with that Redwood National Park, Mr. Collier?

Mr. COLLIER. I am not.

Mr. TAYLOR of North Carolina. If we have history to follow, if our job retraining programs are this disastrous, I am not sure how we can justify spending hundreds of millions of dollars; 10 percent or less job training, was minuscule.

Does anyone have any assessment or any thoughts in that area?

Mr. LYONS. Mr. Taylor, I would point out, unlike the Redwood situation, the economic package, the labor and community assistance package we seek to implement is much more diverse. It addresses some of the issues you raised. It deals with retraining funds, et cetera, but reinvestments in business and industry through low-cost loans and related programs, investments in communities and infrastructure, as well as investments intended to put people back to work in the woods, such as road restoration and watershed maintenance. It is intended to be a much more diverse program, recognizing the diversity of those communities.

I think the social assessments done as a part of this report pointed out something very important. One size does not fit all in terms of the kinds of assistance communities will need. We need to have a broad range of tools to use in providing assistance to those communities.

Mr. TAYLOR of North Carolina. The program in the Redwoods, of course, was lucrative and diverse and had some of the same features.

I would yield back any time left, Mr. Chairman.

Mr. VENTO. Does Mr. DeFazio wish to be recognized for 5 minutes.

Mr. DEFAZIO. Mr. Greber, if we could get into one specific aspect of this. I think the report stands on the credibility of all its parts. And one part I find particularly incredible, so to speak, I don't know if you are responsible, is log export analysis.

Tell me, per million board feet of logs exported, how many jobs are directly related to exports per million board feet of export. You gave us a 16.5 number for a million board feet harvested. Of that, how many jobs are in exports, if that is exported?

There is a great concern here about longshore jobs, and you have come to the conclusion we have an even trade between mill jobs and longshore jobs, which is absurd.

Mr. GREBER. That was never stated in the report. The report says that we are uncertain as to the trade-off between mill jobs and longshore.

Mr. DEFAZIO. So how many jobs do we get in the longshore jobs do we get per million board feet of export?

Mr. GREBER. I do not know.

Mr. DEFAZIO. How many longshore jobs total for the 2 million board feet?

Mr. GREBER. I don't know.

Mr. DEFAZIO. We get 16.5 jobs per million board feet of harvest. Could we safely assume that maybe 1½ of those jobs would go in the export function? How many would we lose in the mill when we export? Of that 16.5, how many of those are in the mill per million?

Mr. GREBER. I have not worked through those types of comparatives. I would be happy to respond after working through those.

Mr. DEFAZIO. So we cannot respond to this. It is an extraordinary assumption.

There has been a lot of discussion of the Bush administration, and I admit he was one of the architects of the train wreck theory and they did a lot of really outrageous stuff, but once they did something good. They would never admit to it, but I managed to get a copy and leak it, Mr. Lyons.

It is titled "Actions the Administration May Wish to Consider in Implementing a Conservation Strategy for the Northern Spotted Owl." The Bush administration told us this did not exist because it was a draft document. So I have a nonexistent draft document written by people at BLM and Ag under the Bush administration, and they assume here that we could get 35,000 jobs in the Northwest by stopping all log exports. Now, somewhere between zero and 35,000 might be the reality.

Why did the administration choose not to address log exports? Honestly? I mean, the Bush administration, as bad as it was, honestly addressed the issue of log exports. This administration, rather incredulously, tells me we cannot gain any jobs by restricting private log exports and we will continue to export 2.57 billion board feet.

And 2.5 million board feet runs through a mill and provides some $x$ number of jobs, and then Dr. Greber cannot tell us——

83

Mr. COLLIER. All I can say is, the administration' made a decision that export policy was a more complicated issue; that we could not address it in this context, and all we did, as you know, was eliminate the FSC payment and that that is the beginning and end of our answer on job exports.

Mr. DEFAZIO. You have another interesting statement in here: What we should do is export high quality logs to existing markets like Japan and China, which totally excludes our finished products, which come from more efficient mills, and we should begin to import logs from Siberia, New Zealand, and Chile.

Now, I would hope that Mr. Lyons, at least, is familiar with the assessment we made of importing Siberian logs. We risk losing all the forest in the Western United States by importing those logs unless we can assure they are pest-free. Again, I would find, for that administration, to be an extraordinary kind of finding to make: Export 2.5 million board feet of high quality timber to countries which in fact discriminate against our finished wood products and go out and become cullinizers ourselves by buying logs from other countries that are falling apart like Russia so that the log ships don't have to sail back empty.

How about we eliminate the log ships? That is a statement more than a question. I understand you are bound by policy.

Let's go to county revenues quickly. I just received this morning a copy of the report. I haven't had a chance to read the whole thing yet, but I am working on it. But in VI–37 we have an estimate of county revenues. My understanding or my concern is that in making these estimates we use a rather low figure.

The stumpage figure of 330—well, $333 per thousand board feet in 1995? Wouldn't that seem low, given the restraints on harvest?

Mr. GREBER. I had first thought, in light of the simulations and the numbers you commonly hear talked about in the press and off the private lands, that yes, that seemed like a low number. I then went back through the Forest Service statistics, and if you look at the average price per thousand board foot across all the products that are taken off the national forest, from thinning volume to cull volume to salvage volume, in 1990 believe it or not, it was as low as $240 a thousand board foot.

It is a lot lower, on average, than we generally think about when we think of saw timber stumpage prices. So we did say $333 per thousand, which did represent about a 30-percent increase in stumpage prices realized on national forests.

So that is based upon Forest Service's own accounting statistics and the price calculation off their accounting statistics.

Mr. DEFAZIO. So using those numbers—I am out of time. I will finish this later.

Mr. VENTO. Mr. Hamburg for 5 minutes.

Mr. HAMBURG. Thank you, Mr. Chairman.

I want to go back again to the issue of the AMA's and again to the Hayfork AMA, which I believe is the largest of the towns. That is about 400,000 acres. And I know the design of the AMA's was so that they would be large enough to be ecologically significant, and that there could be some experimentation that went on, but small enough so that there was a possibility of communities coming together to form plans and ways to best utilize these areas.

I want to ask specifically, though, with respect to the Hayfork AMA and the fact that we were involved with two counties here, two national forests, what went into defining this 400,000 acres. And having some confidence, this could function as a coherent unit of forest management?

Mr. LYONS. I will let Dr. Franklin, who helped lay these out, address that question.

Mr. FRANKLIN. There were a whole series of factors that went into laying them out. One of them was simply geographic distribution, so that we had them well-distributed. Another factor was trying to have a series of areas that represented different kinds of challenges. And in the case of the Hayfork, there was a specific intent here of looking at the Klamath Mountains, and particularly the east side of the Klamath Mountains, providing an area of that kind in that province.

One of the things that we tried to do, and I think we did pretty much avoid with the adaptive management areas, was laying them into any of the critical watersheds, the tier-one watersheds. And, in fact, some area that could have been incorporated in the Hayfork was not, for that reason.

Additionally, we wanted to sort of cradle these adaptive management areas in strong reserves. In other words, they would be bounded by strong reserve systems so that there would be less risk to any regional conservation strategy. So those were all things that went into the design and location.

In addition, as Mr. Lyons pointed out, we did want to try to make them, whenever possible, tributary to communities subject to major impacts as a result of reduced timber harvest. And so those were the factors that went into the design of that area.

Also, obviously, the objective was to provide a coherent ecological unit in terms of watershed boundaries and transportation.

Mr. HAMBURG. Dr. Franklin, what I am concerned about is the size of this. This is an extremely large area, about half the size of Mendocino National Forest and the other, I think almost half the size of Six Rivers. What is that, about 960,000? So this is an extremely large area. And I really don't know where the precedent has been established that areas this large in communities this diverse can come together to do this.

I guess I should hope for the best, but I do have concern, and I didn't see anything specifically in the plan that called for a periodic assessment or evaluation of how well these adaptive management areas are forming these plans and performing according to your expectations.

Mr. FRANKLIN. Mr. Congressman, my personal opinion, it is imperative that there be an oversight mechanism, and that we do build, in fact, very strong monitoring programs into these areas. That was one of the reasons why we suggested that the administration and the Congress might want to consider supplemental funding mechanisms to make sure that that happens.

I would just say one other thing about Hayfork. Hayfork is one of several of the adaptive management areas that includes reserves. So the entire acreage is not, in effect, open to management. It does include some significant acreage as a reserved area.

Mr. HAMBURG. Let me just touch on a related topic, which is the local processing of available timber supply within the areas. And, Jim, I know this is something you have worked on. And in the plan, it talks about the 1990 farm bill as perhaps having sufficient legal authority to make sure that this resource is processed within the area and brings jobs and income to the areas.

Can you comment further on that?

Mr. LYONS. Actually, now that I have a staff of attorneys, the attorneys are looking into what legal authority we have.

I think the important thing to understand here is this is a new way of doing business. It is a mechanism to try and capitalize on the creativity and imagination of those communities. We fully intend, as I mentioned earlier, to establish the monitoring required, the review mechanisms necessary to determine the best way to implement, to establish and implement these adaptive management areas.

As far as legal authority goes, we are looking into that. Whether modifications in existing plans are necessary, we are attempting to make that determination now.

Mr. HAMBURG. Are there precedents for other farm bills used in the past to keep local resources in the local economy?

Mr. LYONS. Not using the 1990 authority, to my knowledge.

Mr. HAMBURG. Thank you, Mr. Chairman.

Mr. VENTO. The time of the gentleman has expired.

Mrs. Unsoeld for 5 minutes.

Mrs. UNSOELD. Thank you, Mr. Chairman.

It was pointed out to me that I was remiss in not thanking the environmentalists for joining in the letter to the court, and I was remiss. I would like to thank them for their cooperation, particularly in light of their early condemnation of option 9, and blame those delegation members from the Northwest as having been the authors of this.

But however delayed, I do appreciate their cooperation at this point and trust and hope that that will bring in a new day in how we get our country moving forward in a more cooperative method and manner. Just as this administration has brought agencies together, hopefully, that path will continue, and you will bring different constituent groups together also in solving those problems.

I just have one question to address to the panel and that is sort of anticipation of problems we are going to have in the future in funding. We have all acknowledged that monitoring was neglected in the past. We even thought that that is not a very good word to call it because it is so hard to get a focus on monitoring.

In the absence of our apparently having come one a better name, Dr. Thomas or anyone else, would you please describe for us our— what our failure to have invested enough in that activity in the past has done to us and why we are really going to need whatever now you want to use in the future?

Mr. J. THOMAS. All human endeavors in natural resource management is a matter of adaptive management. That is a new term, but that is what we have been doing for 100,000 years. As we move very rapidly and as we become more technical, we have to have data on which to make those assessments. That has somewhat been lacking.

It is difficult when somebody says, well, we need to change direction, but it has a cost. And someone says, well, why do we need to change? Well, it looks like things are not working very well. Prove it. And then a prove-it game. It requires monitoring.

Now, in particular, when we take risky courses of action, the idea of monitoring becomes more and more significant. In other words, if we are going to try something, and it is indeed risky, we have to know when we are wrong. We have to know what the trigger points are and we have to know how to move. That is why monitoring is so important.

Previous plans did a very nice job of saying we would monitor, but we have not, at least in terms of scientific opinion, we have not done that as well as we should. I think it is significant, particularly where we take risky courses of action, and to some extent option 9, as pointed out by Mr. Vento, has some risk associated with it.

Therefore, if we choose to take those risks, we should indeed monitor to see that things work as anticipated.

Mr. LYONS. Congresswoman, if I could just amplify. Like Jack said, there are three important points about monitoring that need to be recognized beyond the fact we need to do it. We clearly need to do it. The forest plans each of them versus a monitoring plan which have never been implemented because they have not been funded.

One is with regard to monitoring. We see the potential, I think, for some employment opportunities associated with monitoring; that is, perhaps in an adaptive management area or some other areas there are opportunities to train individuals on the ground, individuals from communities perhaps that have been impacted, to go out and gather some of the basic data that can serve as a basis for analysis to determine how we are doing in implementing and monitoring programs.

Second, is one of the things I hope to be able to come to this committee and to all these committees and request down the road, is some more flexibility in terms of budgeting. More of a results-based budgeting. I think the only way I can justify that is to be able to come up here and demonstrate to you what we are accomplishing for the investments.

So rather than being funded line item by line item and having foresters become accountants, we can allow them to be managers, to monitor what they are doing on the ground and to demonstrate that and justify our budgets.

And, third, monitoring is the key to restoring the credibility of the agencies in the field. We need to be able to demonstrate that we are in fact doing what we have said we are doing, and monitoring certainly is the key there.

Mrs. UNSOELD. Thank you very much.

And thank you, Mr. Chairman.

Mr. VENTO. Thank you. Mr. Condit, are you ready to ask a question of the witnesses at this point.

Mr. CONDIT. Mr. Chairman, first of all, let me apologize for being late. I have just completed chairing a subcommittee or I would have been here earlier.

I don't want to ask any questions that may have already been asked, but I would like permission to submit a statement into the record as well as a letter that I have from a constituent. I would like to be able to submit written questions to the panel in writing, if I may.

Mr. VENTO. Yes. Without objection, the gentleman's requests are made.

Hearing no objections, the prepared statement of Mr. Condit appears at the beginning of the hearing.

Mr. VENTO. I think we are in another round. Peter has a few questions; I have some additional questions. Let's see if we can get through it before the House convenes.

One point I wanted to make, I was fumbling around here when Mr. Farr yielded to me, but in the executive summary of the document of the Forest Ecosystem Management Assessment Team, it points out in here there was some suggestion that the sustained yield levels are going to be less on private lands. It points out that they will be anywhere from 7 to 17 percent below what they have been in the recent 1991, 1992, and, of course, substantially less, about 24 to 32 percent less, than the level during the 1990's.

I was trying to translate that because the suggestion was that somehow the employment figures that we were relying on didn't account for that. In fact, it does account for a substantial drop in terms of employment and with regard to private and public lands, does it not, Dr. Greber?

Mr. GREBER. It counts on the harvest from both the private and public lands, and that harvest level that is used is the average for the first decade. The assumption being 1994 to 2003 on private lands. And that is not a sustainable harvest, and it is a harvest that tapers off throughout the decade. Starts higher and reduces throughout.

Mr. VENTO. I think it is important. Also, you said it would be a long answer, but I want to get the short answer that I understood in terms of your saying that the wood pulp is a long answer, but the short answer is that there are alternative woods such as hardwoods that can be used in wood pulp; is that correct?

Mr. GREBER. Yes. The point is, the pulp and paper industry is made up of the paper industry and the pulp industry. And the reason, there is a large pulp and paper industry of 28,000 employees; 25,000 of them are in paper and paper converting.

With installation of recycle capacity and some of the current market conditions in pulp, it was viewed that the paper jobs over the long term were not of issue. The pulp jobs could be, but it was felt that in the decade ahead, that new pulping technologies and alternative fiber sources, such as hardwoods, could allow those mills to continue to operate.

Mr. VENTO. Whether they hire anyone in the process is another thing. I find that the other phenomena going on here is, even though we have been celebrating the harvest in region 6 during the 1980's for all different types of fiber, the amount of employment has dropped off because of something called automation; is that correct, Dr. Greber?

Mr. GREBER. Employment dropped because of automation significantly from 1980 to 1986.

Mr. VENTO. So there is a phenomenon here in terms of this forest policy land management plan that is receiving a lot of credit for something that probably is occurring extraneous to it, and it is important we all bear that in mind and try to deal with this sort of phenomena as it affects people, and I think that the plan attempts to do that.

The other point, though, in terms of mobilizing the private lands, of course, how will the adaptive management areas, if at all, deal with private lands and those that are intermixed in these instances? Do we have any BLM lands in the adaptive management areas?

Mr. FRANKLIN. Yes. Most of the areas do have a mixture of ownerships, and specifically about one-half of them are a mixture of Bureau of Land Management and Forest Service ownership. And the intent is that the agencies learn how to truly manage those areas as an integrated unit.

Mr. VENTO. This is very encouraging. It didn't dawn on me until I was sitting here this morning that that was the case, even though I have a lot of misgivings about sort of handing this over in terms of walking away from what the forest management or the BLM planning process—resource management plans are, but I think an interesting solution, obviously, too, although it creates some uncertainty.

Isn't it true there are a lot of nonindustrial private forest resource lands that are not being—or potentially wood fiber producing areas that are not now enlisted in such an endeavor?

Mr. FRANKLIN. I think that is true.

Mr. VENTO. So that it would be the plan here to try to utilize them, I take it.

Mr. LYONS. Mr. Chairman, if I could make a point of clarification. Sorry to interrupt, but I want to be clear we are not intending to walk away from the forest planning processes in establishment and implementation of the adaptive management areas.

We are talking about innovative approaches on the ground. We are talking about working with communities to help provide guidance and advice as to how to implement silvicultural systems, et cetera. We still intend to comply with the requirements of the existing law and assure the public at large will have input to the requirements.

Mr. VENTO. Albeit more dynamic, I guess, than what the case word today is: Confrontation. One of the concerns many of us have is the issue of connectivity, and, obviously, the plan does put in place the 15-11-40 in many places.

Can some of you explain in some detail how that might be resolved in terms of leaving some green trees in place, Dr. Thomas?

Mr. J. THOMAS. I invite Jerry Franklin to jump in in a moment, but it depends on where you are in the Northwest region.

There are different prescriptions for handling the matrix. In some cases, we are talking about, in the Cascade range we are talking, I believe, 15 percent retention with one-half of that in clumps of about four-tenths of an acre. Otherwise, where there is a considerable substitution of riparian zone protection areas, the substitute for the 15-11-40 rule in the matrix.

So it varies, given circumstances across the range.

Mr. VENTO. Now, my time has expired. I appreciate the patience of my colleagues. Congressman DeFazio.

Mr. DeFazio. I thank the gentleman. We have been contacted by the O&C counties and they have raised concerns about the percentage guarantees. I would just like to pursue a course of questioning here that relates to that.

Mr. Collier, my understanding is BLM volume under contract is about 330 million board feet. What do you expect will be remaining as of October 1 next year? Can you give me a number? How much would there be left to harvest in the next fiscal year on BLM land?

Mr. Collier. I am not sure what that number is, Congressman. I am sorry.

Mr. DeFazio. Let's say one-half, OK? Do you know what the value of that is?

Mr. Collier. I do not.

Mr. DeFazio. Then we will go back to Mr. Greber and the world of academics here. You said that you have looked at all the species.

Do you have a breakdown between BLM and the Forest Service on that or do you aggregate the two?

Mr. Greber. The harvest on BLM and the harvest on——

Mr. DeFazio. For the valuation you have reached on stumps.

Mr. Greber. Yes.

Mr. DeFazio. That was assuming—essentially assuming similar characteristics. Do you know anything about the characteristics of what is proposed to be harvested on BLM lands that would make you raise that estimate dramatically for the stumpage value?

I mean, you are assuming a mix. Is there a unique—I mean, is there more high value stuff that is going to come out of BLM lands, are you aware?

Mr. Greber. I am not aware of exactly what the proportionate split would be, what the ratio would be.

Mr. DeFazio. Dr. Johnson, are you aware of the timber characteristics on BLM lands, what is proposed to be harvested under this plan and whether or not it is basically—would you agree with what Dr. Greber's conclusions are about stumpage values?

Can you average them that way or do you think they would be a lot higher on BLM lands?

Mr. Johnson. I agree generally with Dr. Greber. BLM tend to be lower elevation, closer to market, might have a slightly higher value.

Mr. DeFazio. So maybe we should bump it up some more over the 333.

OK, so the interesting point is that the counties would like to have either/or, and I would like to have either/or too just in case, but when we look at the or, assuming the or is their traditional share of value, under the chart on page VI–37, we find that we are projecting a county share of $42 million as opposed to an historic 1990 to 1992 of $131 million. That is about a 60- to 70-percent decrease in revenues.

So if we doubled Dr. Greber's stumpage estimates, disregarding the mix that you are talking about, but—I would assume it would be—I mean, if we go wild here, we could double it, right? So that would get us up to 82, which is considerably less than the administration is offering in the 85 percent, even until we get 4 or 5 years out.

So I would just like to make that point. But to get back to Mr. Collier, are you conversant with this either/or dispute? The understanding is that Mr. Yew in conversations I was not privy to told the counties either/or and now they are being told that is it. Are you conversant with that?

Mr. COLLIER. My understanding is that is it.

Mr. DEFAZIO. That is it, OK. Was that your understanding—did Mr. Yew misspeak himself previously?

Mr. COLLIER. I didn't know what the policy decision was at the time he spoke, so I don't know whether he misspoke or not.

Mr. DEFAZIO. So you are saying the administration at this point would not consider an either/or?

Mr. COLLIER. That is correct, Congressman.

Mr. DEFAZIO. Why is that? Is that the policy?

Mr. COLLIER. OMB folks and the rest of them working on it have decided that that is the best course for us to take.

Mr. DEFAZIO. Well, it is interesting.

Mr. COLLIER. Congressman, we are providing a significant relief for the O&C counties. I think a lot of us put a great deal of effort in that. I know you have helped with that effort, but I would, given your questions, I would just hope we not lose sight of the fact that we have provided significant relief for those counties——

Mr. DEFAZIO. No, I am not about to look $270 million in the face and say, oh, thank you very much, but I want to stand on a principle here that will give me 30 percent of that over the next 5 years. No, I am not taking that position, but I am trying to work through a problem with the counties and part of the problem is perception, and if I look at your chart here, it wouldn't cost you anything to give us an either/or because you are projecting that under the or, we are only going to get a third of our normal revenues.

So, maybe just sort of accommodate us with an or when, in fact, you know, we are not going to exercise it because it would mean a dramatic reduction in the revenues we would receive.

Mr. COLLIER. The decision is out of my hands.

Mr. DEFAZIO. Who do you think I ought to talk to? Leon Panetta?

Mr. COLLIER. Yes, sir.

Mr. DEFAZIO. OK, thank you.

Mr. VENTO. Well, the gentleman has——

Mr. DEFAZIO. I have other questions, but not with the yellow light on. I can't get them done.

Mr. VENTO. Actually the yellow indicates you have about a minute. But in any case, I have conferred with Congresswoman Unsoeld and she has exhausted her questions and I have.

Mr. DEFAZIO. Mr. Chairman, if I could quickly, there is a question of statutory authority here and this would mean to me sort of a second instance—Mr. Chairman, could I have 1 additional minute?

Mr. VENTO. Certainly. Without objection, the gentleman is recognized for an additional minute.

Mr. DEFAZIO. There is a question of statutory authority here and this would be to me the second time we have seen sort of a waiver of statutory authority by the administration.

I have already discussed previously with Mr. Collier the issue of the NFMA viability requirement and the extension of BLM lands. We don't have time to get into that.

This would be sort of secondary. I mean, there is a statutory provision, so—that provides these guarantees. It has been longstanding, 60 years just about, so, again——

Mr. COLLIER. Where is the waiver, Congressman? What we are providing is relief as to those counties over and above what the statute would require, given the timber that is going to be cut.

Mr. DEFAZIO. Right.

Mr. COLLIER. I don't see a statutory waiver.

Mr. DEFAZIO. So you are saying if the guarantee exceeds what they would have received under the formula established by law, then in fact unless they want to sue to receive less they would have to take more?

Mr. COLLIER. That is correct, Congressman.

Mr. DEFAZIO. All right.

Mr. Chairman, thank you.

Mr. VENTO. I thank the gentleman.

I would just put into the record, without objection, the letter to Mr. Victor Sher and Todd True with the Sierra Club Legal Defense Fund, the issue as referred to. I would just point out that the document indicates the willingness that the information—or the willingness of the administration to identify in timber sale volume and release from the existing injunction *Seattle Audubon Society* versus *Lyons.*

I believe that is Assistant Secretary Lyons, whose name has been transferred to this from his successor, his predecessor, pardon me, and furthermore, it goes on to point out that the administration will continue to resist sufficiency that is the circumvention of the existing body of environmental and other law, which of course has been a commitment since entering this process to try to work within the law, which I think is the right policy path, notwithstanding that there may be from time to time minor changes or adjustments that are made in Congress.

And so I think this is really a major step forward in terms of a good faith effort to free up salable timber, provide something in the pipeline which is running close to empty and keep in place the viability at least, as well as can be expected of those vitally dependent upon that, on timber in the Pacific Northwest.

With that I have no further questions, and I want to thank the members and staff for their cooperation. The meeting stands adjourned.

[Whereupon, at 1:20 p.m., the subcommittees were adjourned, to reconvene, subject to the call of the Chair.]

[Material submitted for inclusion in the record follows:]

**Statement of Tom Collier,**
**Chief of Staff to Interior Secretary Bruce Babbitt**
**Before a Joint Hearing**
**Of the House Natural Resources Subcommittee**
**on National Parks, Forests, and Public Lands;**
**House Agriculture Subcommittee**
**on Specialty Crops and Natural Resources;**
**and the House Merchant Marine and Fisheries Subcommittee**
**on Environment and Natural Resources**
**August 3, 1992**

Good morning, Chairmen, and members of the Committees. My name is Tom Collier. I am Chief of Staff for Interior Secretary Babbitt and I appear here on behalf of the Department. I want to thank you for the opportunity to testify this morning on the President's Forest Management Plan.

I want to describe some of the basic elements of the President's proposed plan, but I wish primarily to describe how we got here. Without that context, it is difficult to understand the dilemma -- and how we managed to anger so many people with the President's plan. I will focus on policies and actions of the last half-dozen years, but am well aware that the crisis we are in developed through 20 years of federal policies since the first warnings about threats to the Northern spotted owl, policies over 50 years since the invention of the gas-powered chain saw, and policies spanning more than a century of logging.

This context is essential to understanding the President's proposal, which is a clean and unequivocal break from past approaches to this growing problem.

The history of Federal forest management in the Pacific Northwest over the last decade is one of short-sightedness and deliberate procrastination, and deliberate overharvesting and deliberate indifference to recommendations by career civil servants, Federal laws and the courts. The government knew it was cutting too much timber: there were numerous reputable warnings. And the judges that intervened were not overzealous: on the contrary, they would probably have agreed to reasonable government requests. The government's approach was to deliberately become boxed in by environmental laws so as to convince Congress that those laws needed changing. The strategy failed. The price of that failure is being paid by the people of the region, particularly those in the small logging communities whose workers depend on the federal forests.

Had this crisis been dealt with earlier, we might have been able to devise a plan with more timber for harvest and more protected areas. But we follow years of avoidance. Secretary Babbitt has spoken often of avoiding environmental "train wrecks." It is too late for that; we are dealing with the aftermath of a horrible train wreck. The passengers victimized are timber workers who have lost their jobs over the past two years; mills that have shut down; families that have lost their homes, their dreams, and any faith they had in the federal government. They are salmon fishermen who have seen the stocks dwindle year after year, and native tribes who have tried to manage their own resources only to have those resources threatened by mismanagement of the resources of others.

## A Litany of Legal Warnings

How did this happen? How could the federal agencies have missed the writing on the wall? They simply ignored it. It is, quite simply, too much to believe that the loud and harsh warnings from Federal judges went unheard. Most people have heard only of a U.S. District Court judge named William Dwyer, the lightning rod for critics of the laws at issue here: the National Forest Management Act (NFMA), the National Environmental Policy Act (NEPA) and the Endangered Species Act. But the Federal judges who have ruled against the government in timber sale cases over the past five years could field a baseball team with players to spare. Zilly. Frye. Jones. Choy. Schroeder. Nelson. Goodwin. Pregerson. Marsh. All said the government was violating the law. The Administration's claim: the rulings were unclear.

When Judge Dwyer, in a 1991 decision, accused the Forest Service of "a remarkable series of violations of the environmental laws," he no doubt thought he was speaking with clarity, for there is a long string of violations.

In 1987, the BLM developed a conservation plan for its lands in the region, using environmental impact statements prepared prior to 1983. This, despite the fact that, in the ensuing years, the Fish and Wildlife Service had done a new status review, the Forest Service had drafted a supplemental EIS, a blue ribbon panel of scientists had completed an owl study, a leading scientist had published a population demographics and viability review, and the BLM's own biologists had done a new owl report. The obvious result: District Judge Helen Frye held the BLM in violation of NEPA. The BLM lost its appeal of that decision, with the judges describing the BLM record as a "deliberate, protracted refusal to comply with applicable environmental laws."

In 1988, the Fish and Wildlife Service arbitrarily refused to consider a petition for listing a species as endangered. Judge Thomas Zilly overruled the Service and forced it to consider the petition for the spotted owl, which eventually was listed.

The Fish and Wildlife Service is required by statute to take action regarding critical habitat when it does list a species. In 1991, Judge Zilly had to spell it out. He said the Service "abused its discretion when it determined not to designate critical habitat concurrently with the listing of the northern spotted owl, or to explain any basis for concluding that the critical habitat was not determinable. These actions were arbitrary and capricious, and contrary to law."

The government issued a strategy to protect the owl and it was required to first run it by the Fish and Wildlife Service for suggestions. The Administration refused to do so, which is why, in 1992, District Judge Robert Jones threw out the so-called "Jamison Strategy" and demanded consultation. The government's response? It appealed. It lost.

In each court case, at each step, the executive branch was told exactly what the courts required, ignored the admonitions, ignored deadlines, and was slapped with injunctions. Judge Dwyer's conclusion: "more is involved here than a simple failure by an agency to comply with its governing statute. The most recent violation of NFMA exemplifies a deliberate and systematic refusal by the Forest Service and the FWS to comply with the laws protecting wildlife. This is not the doing of the scientists, foresters, rangers, and others at the working levels of these agencies. It reflects decisions made by higher authorities in the executive branch of government."

## Consistent Scientific Warnings

The legal community was not alone in pointing out the growing crisis. There were ample scientific warnings, throughout the mid- to late-1980s, that harvest levels were unsustainable.

Jim Torrence, former chief forester in Region Six, said that

20 percent harvest reductions -- to four billion board feet per year -- would not come close to making the harvest levels sustainable. As supervisor of the Mount Baker National Forest in Washington state, he asked for permission to lower the annual sales quantity; he was turned down.

In 1989, Purdue University Forestry Chair Dennis LeMaster warned that "there are limits in what can be expected of them in terms of resource yields. These limits have been reached in the Pacific Northwest. We may want certainty in timber output levels, but given their current level and the other requirements imposed on the national forests, we are very optimistic to expect it."

In 1990, an Interagency team of government scientists agreed. The Interagency Scientific Committee said that the lack of a consistent planning strategy had resulted in a high risk of extinction for the owl. The Forest Service, which initially planned to adopt the ISC Report, was told by the Administration to develop an alternative.

## A Narrow Range of Options

This litany of denials -- of ignored warnings and callous delays -- is important in understanding where we are today. It is, quite simply, the context in which you must judge the President's proposal. It is the reason why the range of options for the President was, in fact, so very small.

Very few people expected a return to cut levels of five billion board feet. At the same time, very few expected a ten-year average annual sales quantity figure of 1.2 billion board feet. To be honest, neither did we. We had some very reasonable people telling us they would support the plan if it provided two billion or more board feet. At the time, we were pleased with that "line in the sand," because we thought it achievable.

The fact is, however, another clear warning has been issued: according to the best science we have today, the timber just isn't there to sustain a higher level. We cannot continue to ignore warnings such as these.

We know this plan will cause some additional injuries, and we deeply regret that. Years of denial have made this problem worse; considerable interest has compounded the bill we must now pay. This President has stepped up to the task. His proposed Forest Ecosystem Management Plan represents a fundamental shift in land management philosophy, away from the artificial political and jurisdictional boundaries that have constrained our approaches in the past, to a philosophy based on nature's own boundaries. The plan will prove to be a historically significant proposal, constituting a major turning point in public land management.

The plan reflects the President's directive that his Cabinet secretaries end the fistfights between agencies and that those involved in this issue work together and as one. That goal is achieved. We have disagreements, surely, but we talk them out and find consensus.

The plan represents the best scientific information available on what is needed to protect the biological diversity of our Federal forest lands. Some argue -- as the previous Administrations did -- that we should throw out the science and make the policy decision to cut more timber. They claim we are ignoring economics. The President is acutely aware that the anticipated yields from these lands are lower than he would have liked to see. But there is no free lunch. The plan is not just what is needed according to science, but also according to sound economic management. Overcutting has made the situation worse: continuing down that road would add even more interest to the "eventual debt. The solution is better long-term management, not the forestry equivalent of deficit spending.

As hard as the Forest Ecosystem Management Assessment Team worked on it, the plan we have presented probably isn't perfect. It is, and ought to be, subject to adjustment over the short term and the long term. The ambitiousness of the scientific undertaking --

to craft a land management regime covering three states, millions of acres and literally thousands of species -- cannot be overestimated. On some specific items, the level of information is enormous and the degree of certainty high. On others, we simply don't know as much as we would like. We have made the best judgments we can with the information we have, and we commit ourselves to learning more. The ecosystem management plan is designed for change, anticipates change, and no doubt will need change. We will get better at the management of complex ecosystems, and as we do, we will adjust details of the plan. Some criticize the absence of a broad-based system of permanent, immutable reserves; to create such a reserve would presume a degree of knowledge that in many instances is simply not there.

We are moving forward rapidly. The Secretaries of Agriculture, Interior, Labor and Commerce and the Administrator of the Environmental Protection Agency, under the direction of the Director of the White House Office of Environmental Policy, are working together to develop procedures for implementing a forest management plan. These agencies are also cooperating, under the direction of the National Economic Council, in the preparation of a community assistance package.

This plan represents a new way of addressing this complex problem and a new covenant between government agencies. The Forest Service and the BLM will join with the Fish and Wildlife Service to form consultation teams to achieve new efficiencies in Endangered Species Act implementation. The Fish and Wildlife Service and the National Marine Fisheries Service scientists will be working with foresters in the field, to ensure things are done right the first time around. The federal government will ask state, local and tribal governments to join together to design long-term forest plans. Timber will move faster to market because the agencies will not be falling over each other.

I have said much about the past. We need to move forward, laying out the plan for the future instead of expending energy trying to repair past mistakes. Our wish is to usher in a profoundly new era in land management in the Northwest, for the good of the region's environment and its economy.

In closing, I would like to tell members of these Committees that this has been an extraordinary exercise. Assistant Secretary Lyons, I believe, will agree that we did not know how difficult a project this would be when the President convened the Forest Conference in Portland in April. We did not know the extent of the limitations that the past would impose on us, nor did we realize just how grave the threats to the natural bounty of the Northwest are. If it was not already apparent that bold action was required, it became very clear to us quickly. Our work has been consistent and steady because of the commitments we have made. We take very seriously the commitment we have made to the people of the

Northwest.  And we take very seriously the President's commitment
to a reasonable and balanced solution.

I thank you for listening, and for holding this joint hearing.
I look forward to answering any questions you may have.

STATEMENT OF
JAMES LYONS, ASSISTANT SECRETARY
NATURAL RESOURCES AND ENVIRONMENT
UNITED STATES DEPARTMENT OF AGRICULTURE

Before the
Subcommittee on National Parks and Public Lands
Committee on Natural Resources
Subcommittee on Specialty Crops and Natural Resources
Committee on Agriculture
and the
Subcommittee on Environment and Natural Resources
Committee on Merchant Marine and Fisheries
United States House of Representatives

Concerning the Administration's Proposed Northwest Timber Policy

August 3, 1993

Mr. Chairmen and Members of the Subcommittees, I am James R.
Lyons, Assistant Secretary for Natural Resources and Environment of
the U.S. Department of Agriculture. I am pleased to join Mr. Tom
Collier, Chief of Staff of the U.S. Department of the Interior in
appearing before you today to discuss the President's Forest Ecosystem
Management Plan for the Pacific Northwest.

Also joining us today are members of the Forest Ecosystem
Management Assessment Team (FEMAT) who developed the forest management
report which serves as the basis for the President's plan.
Specifically, we are joined by Dr. Jack Ward Thomas, who served as
Team Leader; Dr. James Sedell, who co-chaired the Aquatic/Watershed
Group; Dr. K. Norman Johnson, leader of the Resource Analysis Group;
Dr. Brian Greber, leader of the Economic Assessment Group; and Dr.
Roger Clark, who led the Social Assessment Group.

Overview

At the conclusion of the Forest Conference in Portland, Oregon,
President Clinton outlined five principles to guide the work of the
Administration in crafting a solution to the forest management
conundrum that faces the Pacific Northwest and northern California.
The President stated:

"First, we must never forget the human and the economic dimensions
of these problems.  Where sound management policies can preserve the
health of forest lands, sales should go forward.  Where this
requirement cannot be met, we need to do our best to offer new
economic opportunities for year-round, high-wage, high-skill jobs.

Second, as we craft a plan, we need to protect the long-term
health of our forests, our wildlife, and our waterways.  They are a
gift from God, and we hold them in trust for future generations.

Third, our efforts must be, insofar as we are wise enough to know
it, scientifically sound, ecologically credible, and legally
responsible.

Fourth, the plan should produce a predictable and sustainable
level of timber sales and nontimber resources that will not degrade or
destroy the environment.

Fifth, to achieve these goals, we will do our best...to make the Federal government work together and work for you. We may make mistakes, but we will try to end the gridlock within the Federal government, and we will insist on collaboration, not confrontation."

The President established a number of working groups to develop options and approaches for achieving these objectives.

The Labor and Community Assistance Working Group was charged with the development of tools to aid individuals and communities affected by changes in Federal and private forest land management in the region. Their work identified a 5-year, $1.2 billion assistance program to offset job losses from reductions in Federal timber harvests, to aid in the development of new business, to assist communities in diversifying their economic bases, and promote the development of new jobs in the region.

The Agency Coordination Working Group devised a new strategy for promoting cooperation and collaboration among the Federal agencies entrusted with the management of the region's renewable natural resources. The President's plan incorporates key elements of this strategy, providing for the establishment of regional interagency representatives to coordinate the implementation of the forestry plan, to develop a common natural resource data base for future management, and to establish watershed management as the basis for integrated resource management and planning in the future.

My remarks this morning, Mr. Chairmen, will focus on the
activities of the third working group that the President established,
the Forest Ecosystem Managment Assessment Team.

## Background

As my colleague Mr. Collier, has already indicated, the history of
this issue is strewn with the wreckage of failed attempts to devise
and implement a managment strategy that is legally sound and/or
politically acceptable. Neither previous Administrations nor the
Congress has been able to construct a resolution which could either
pass muster with the courts or find sufficient political support to
permit its passage by the Congress and enactment into law. Many of
the Members at this dais, including two of the three Subcommittee
Chairmen here today, have invested a great deal of time and energy in
seeking to develop a resolution to this issue.

In fact, the most promising Congressional effort to date was the
product of the collaborative effort of the Chairmen of the three House
Committees and the subcommittees who have convened this hearing
today.

That collaborative effort generated H.R. 4899 in the 102nd
Congress, a measure that successfully passed the Committee on
Agriculture, only to stall later in the legislative process. That
bill, in fact, has many elements in common with the President's Forest
Plan.

First, both the resource management stratey embodied in H.R. 4899
and the President's plan are based on scientificially-sound,
ecosystem-oriented set of forest management principles.  In short, the
strategy embodied in H.R. 4899 and the President's plan sought to move
from the species-by-species protection approach of the past to an
integrated, multi-species management framework - one that would, as
your former Congressman Sid Morrison stated, eliminate the "endangered
species of the month" problem.  Second, the management options which
served as the basis for both H.R. 4899 and those which underly the
President's plan were devised by a team of individuals with expertise
in forest ecosystems, wildlife management, fisheries biology,
hydrology, silviculture, and forest economics.  This
multi-disciplinary approach is essential to understanding the
biological, social, and economic ramifications of the strategy
selected.  Third, in both instances the options ranged from those that
provided higher levels of timber production and, concurrently, lesser
protection for old-growth ecosystems and associated plant and animal
species, to those which protected most, if not all, remaining old
growth, yielding much less timber.  Thus both the President and the
congressional authors of H.R. 4899 had a wide range of
scientifically-based options from which to choose.  And finally, as in
the "Gang of Four" exercise which led to the introduction of
H.R. 4899, the FEMAT generated options for the President's
consideration but did not choose an alternative.  That decision was
left to the policymakers.

The charge given to the FEMAT by President Clinton was clearly articulated in a letter of instruction to the team. Specifically, FEMAT was instructed to identify management alternatives that attain the greatest economic and social contribution from the forests of the region and meet the requirements of the applicable laws and regulations, including the Endangered Species Act, the National Forest Management Act, the Federal Land Policy Management Act, and the National Environmental Policy Act. In short, the team was instructed to identify alternative management strategies that minimized social and economic hardship in complying with applicable forestry and environmental laws.

## The Scientific Basis for FEMAT

FEMAT's work benefited from a substantial body of information and analysis stemming from previous efforts to address the various management issues affecting the region.

Specifically, the team benefited from the report of the Interagency Spotted Owl Committee (ISC) and the draft report of the Recovery Team for the Northern Spotted Owl, two reports developed under guidance of the Bush Administration. In addition, FEMAT used information generated by the Scientific Analysis Team (SAT) which developed a strategy for protecting over 1400 old-growth associated fish and wildlife species and the PACFISH report which charts a strategy for the conservation and management of anadromous fisheries resources in the region. Finally, FEMAT utilized the work of the so-called "Gang of Four" which, under the guidance of the House Agriculture and Merchant Marine and Fisheries Committees, identified alternatives for management of late-successional old-growth forest ecosystems in the Pacific Northwest and northern California.

With these scientific studies as a foundation, the FEMAT expanded the scope of its analysis, further refining the more than 40 management options reflected in these prior reports, and identifying a new set of alternatives.

Some have criticized the work of FEMAT and the composition of the scientific team. Contrary to these criticisms, this team was not simply the "same old scientists". Instead, it represented a mix of those with experience and expertise from these efforts with new individuals with new and different expertise. This was an interagency team, with experts from the Forest Service, Fish and Wildlife Service, Bureau of Land Management, National Marine Fisheries Service, and Environmental Protection Agency represented. Additional expertise from the University of Washington, Washington State University, Oregon State University, University of California, and other academic institutions was also represented. It was a multidisciplinary team, including ecology and forestry. The team also included forest planners and managers - not only researchers and scientists - from national forests and BLM districts in the region.

## The Process of Developing the Ecosystem Management Options

The FEMAT evaluated a range of 58 options for management of
old-growth forests in Oregon, Washington, and northern California.  Of
primary concern was the need to comply with the viability requirements
of the National Forest Management Act and to ensure that management
needs of threatened species, including the northern spotted owl and
the marbled murrelet and listed stocks of anadromous fish species,
were met.  Using strategies devised from earlier studies, a new set of
ten management options was developed.

For each of these options, assessments were conducted to determine
how the viability of key species of fish and wildlife might be
affected.  In all, the viability of over 1400 species was evaluated,
either individually or by group.  Initial viability ratings were made
by panels of experts who had knowledge of a particular species
(e.g.,owls) or group of species (e.g.,mollusks).  These viability
ratings were reviewed subsequently by members of the FEMAT and further
adjustments made to reflect their collective expertise.

After an initial review of options developed by the FEMAT, the team decided to develop several additional options. These options were designed to achieve multiple management objectives more efficiently and to use watersheds as the basic framework for creating a reserve system. In addition, and most importantly, these options were built upon the current management direction for BLM and national forest management plans and then added additional protections as were necessary to achieve stated conservation objectives. Option nine, the basis for the President's Forest Plan, was constructed in this manner.

## The Case for Option Nine

Option nine - the basis for the President's Forest Plan - represents a new approach to forest ecosystem management which recognizes first and foremost that watershed management and the protection of riparian areas are critical elements for sustainable forest management in the region. While prior strategies such as the ISC report and the recovery plan for the northern spotted owl were designed to protect owls, the scientific team recognized that attention to watersheds, both for their importance to water quality and critical fisheries, is key to effective multiple-resource management in the region.

Watersheds are the foundation for the conservation strategy embodied in option nine. More efficient use of reserves could be achieved when they were designed in conjunction with key watersheds and modified to achieve other objectives, such as protecting spotted owls. In addition, as riparian area protections were incorporated into the strategy, management prescriptions for lands outside the reserve-i.e., in the management matrix-could be eased. It is for this reason that option nine does not require application of the "50-11-40" rule in harvesting timber in the matrix. Connectivity is achieved, instead, through maintenance of riparian corridors. The "50-11-40" rule requires 50 percent of forested land within each quarter township to have trees averaging at least 11 inches in diameter at breast height and with a stand canopy closure of at least 40 percent.

Greater flexibility for management of lands in the reserves is also provided under option nine. Thinning of young forest stands-up to 80-years of age - is provided as a means of enhancing and accelerating the development of old-growth forest characteristics. In addition, salvage of timber is permitted in the reserves provided such timbering has a neutral or positive effect on the management objectives of the reserves, as determined by a scientific panel.

Key watersheds designated under option nine are intended to guide future management activities to ensure that sensitive fish stocks and critical water quality areas are not harmed. Analysis of these watersheds will be conducted to guide timbering and other management activities to ensure that these resource management goals are achieved.

A unique aspect of option nine is the creation of adaptive management areas. These units, ranging in size from 80,000 to 480,000 acres are intended to promote the development of innovative management strategies to achieve conservation goals and to encourage greater public participation in deciding how these forests might be managed. This new approach to management is intended to recognize that people are critical components of forest ecosystems and to capitalize on their imagination and resourcefulness in deciding future management policy and direction.

## Timber Sale Levels and Option Nine

Much has been made of the anticipated annual sale quantities that would result from implementation of option nine. Some clarification is warranted.

First, it is important to recognize that it is highly unlikely that current levels of timber harvest from the region are sustainable if the Forest Service is to comply with existing requirements for multiple-use, sustained-yield management in the region. Option 7 of the FEMAT report approximates current direction that might be implemented if the federal agencies continued present land and resource management planning processes and if they were to adopt the elements of the Final Draft Recovery Plan for the Northern Spotted Owl. If implemented, this option would yield 1.15 billion board feet annually (for the northern spotted owl region), compared to 2.6 bbf for the final forest plans. However, viability ratings for the marbled murrelet would be low and for fish species even lower. It would therefore appear that current management direction would fail the requirements for maintaining viability on national forest system lands.

It is also important to recognize that a number of factors have led to overly optimistic projections of allowable sale quantities in the past. The projected annual sale quantity estimates under this analysis sought to correct those. In fact, rather than report an estimated annual sale quantity (ASQ), the FEMAT provides an estimate of the PSQ or probable sale quantity.

The distinctions are important. ASQs represent estimated ceilings for harvest levels for each national forest planning unit. They were intended to be the theoretical maximum level that could be harvested. That was fine for forest planning purposes. But problems arose when some ASQs were interpreted as targets instead of ceilings. As a result, unrealistic expectations of sustainable harvest levels have been set. As verified by individual forests and the FEMAT, it is highly unlikely that recent levels of harvest can be sustained.

PSQs are intended to reflect realistic expectations of what can be harvested on the ground. Further analysis on a unit by unit basis will be needed to verify sustainable harvest levels. However, the PSQs are an honest attempt to reduce confusion between past projections and current estimates of what can actually be harvested on an annual sustained-yield basis.

Implementation of the President's Forest Plan

The President's Forest Management Plan for the region was
presented to Judge Dwyer on July 16th as the preferred alternative in
the Draft Supplemental EIS for the Regional Guide for Management of
the Northern Spotted Owl.  In addition, last week the document was
issued for public review and comment.

A final plan will not be in place, should the current schedule be
followed, until the end of this year.  However, to the extent
feasible, the Administration is moving forward to use the strategy in
its present form to guide planning for future management activities.
Should changes in the document occur as a result of public comment,
further adjustments will be made accordingly.

A key to implementation is coordination and cooperation among the
affected federal agencies.  Last week, a regional interagency
coordination team was established in Portland to facilitate
development of management activities in the short term in conjunction
with the President's plan and to begin the process of establishing the
mechanisms for more efficient and effective resource management in the
region in the future.

As a part of this effort, a review of all existing enjoined timber sales is being conducted to determine what modifications, if any, may be needed to expedite their preparation and sale. We are considering approaching the Court to seek a partial lifting of the injunction. We hope that this process will permit us to move more timber, sooner than would be required if we had to wait for the SEIS to be finalized in December.

I should also point out, Mr. Chairman, that the long term implementation of the President's Forest Plan will require revision and modification of individual forest plans. The FEMAT report acknowledges this, calling for refinement in the basic conservation strategy at the forest level. An important part of this refinement is analysis of individual watersheds to determine where timber harvesting is appropriate and modifications in riparian area protections are warranted. It is also important to note that the BLM resource management plans and the Forest Service's Region 5 forest plans in the owl region are largely consistent with option nine in their present form. We anticipate that only minor modification of these plans will be needed to facilitate implementation.

## Summary

In summary, Mr. Chairman, I would like to make the case for why this forest management strategy-the President's Forest Plan-is the right thing to do!

First, the people of the region and their communities need this issue resolved. For too long they have been given promises, they've been told to hold on and hold out, and they have only suffered as a result. Mr. Chairman, the people who reside in these rural communities have been used like pawns in a game of political chess, pitting agency against agency, industry against labor, and government against the people they are supposed to serve. The people caught in the middle are rightfully fed up. We owe them a resolution to the issue. The President has put forward a bold, innovative, and yes, controversial plan to attempt to bring this issue to closure. But let's not kid ourselves. If this issue had been easier to resolve, Congress and the Bush administration would have done so. This President is willing to make the tough choices and provide the leadership needed to successfully end the logjam.

Second, this plan is balanced. I know that our critics look at a 1.2 bbf annual sale quantity, compare it to the harvest levels of the mid-80's and say, "This is balance?". I must admit, Mr. Chairmen, having worked with many of you on this issue over the past 6 or 7 years, those numbers are shocking in comparison to the harvest levels of the last decade. However, we realize now that we were cutting timber faster than we could sustain. This plan is balanced because it seeks to maintain a sustainable federal timber harvest level without compromising the other natural resources we are entrusted to manage. In addition, we believe the Forest Plan can provide the basis for substantive relief from the current constraints on private forest lands in the region. The plan does not protect all remaining old growth. If we are to have a timber supply in the region for the foreseeable future, some of it will have to be cut. The plan protects the old growth that is needed to secure the future of owls, murrelets, fish, and the old-growth ecosystem, while providing for a sustained

timber harvest. This is a rational way to proceed. In fact, it is
the only way to proceed in a legally-responsible and rational way.

Finally, Mr. Chairmen, I would argue that this plan is sound and
credible because it is firmly based upon our knowledge of forestry and
forest ecosystems and the way in which forestry affects the resources
we are entrusted to manage. Some people have criticized the science
and the scientists who are part of FEMAT. These critics argue, "This
isn't science." And they are right. The FEMAT report isn't science
in the traditional sense. It's the product of the collective
expertise of the best scientists we could assemble, attempting to
construct a regional management plan the likes of which has never been
created before.

I don't believe that we want scientists making the kinds of policy
calls that were made in selecting option nine. That's the role of the
President, and the Congress, and people like you and me.

What we do want, however, is for the policy decisions that we make
to be based on the best information we have. Our role is to take that
information and use it to make informed and responsible judgements
about what our policies ought and ought not to be.

I believe, Mr. Chairmen, that we have done our job in providing the President with the best information available. And, I would submit that he has done his job and fulfilled his commitment to develop a plan to end the logjam that has paralyzed the region.

Thank you for the opportunity to offer my views. We will gladly respond to your questions regarding the President's forest plan and its development.

Statement by
Dr. K. Norman Johnson
Department of Forest Resources
Oregon State University

at a hearing of Subcommittees on
National Parks, Forests and Public Lands (Natural Resource Comm.);
Specialty Crops and Natural Resources (Agriculture Comm.); and
Environment and Natural Resources (Merchant Marine and Fisheries
Comm.)
House of Representatives
US Congress

August 3, 1993

I am Dr. K. Norman Johnson, Professor of Forest Resources at Oregon
State University. I recently led the estimation of sustainable
harvest levels for the Forest Ecosystem Management Assessment Team
(FEMAT). In this statement, I will briefly summarize my findings
from that assessment:

1) With the assistance of Forest Service and BLM personnel, I
projected the sustainable harvest level for each National Forest
and BLM Master Unit in the owl region under each of the 10 FEMAT
options. In this assessment, I ask that Forest Service and BLM
analysts estimate the likely level of sustainable harvest under
each option. We called this estimate the "probable sale quantity"
in the FEMAT Report to distinguish it from the "allowable sale
quantity" of previous assessments and the forest plans. Those
previous assessments, at least for the Forest Service, estimated
ceiling (upper limit) harvest levels. Thus, in this effort, we
attempted to portray the likely sales level under each option
(probable sale quantity) as opposed to an upper limit (allowable
sale quantity) as often done in the past.

2) In our assessment, we estimated the probable sale quantity for
lands on which timber harvest can regularly be scheduled. Thus, we
excluded Congressional withdrawals, administrative withdrawals (in
the forest plans), late-successional reserves, and riparian
reserves from this estimate. After reducing the land base from
these withdrawals and reserves, we are left with "matrix" lands
and, in at least one option, with adaptive management areas. For
purposes of calculating sustainable harvest levels, we also
excluded physically unsuitable lands scattered through matrix lands
and adaptive management areas. Thus the timber base assumed in our
calculations will be less than the total area in the matrix +
adaptive management areas. In a separate calculation, we estimated
potential thinning and catastrophic salvage from the late
successional reserves, but we did not include that estimate in our
estimates of the probable sale quantity.

3) We first estimated the probable sale level for the forest plans plus the recovery plan for the northern spotted owl---what might be called "existing policy". This estimate came out considerably lower than previous estimates of the timber harvest level compatible with owl protection (especially for Region 6) and created quite a stir, including national press coverage. In the next few paragraphs, I will attempt to explain how and why these results occurred.

Over the last three years, the Forest Service in Region 6 has made a substantial downward revision in the harvest level compatible with a scientifically credible plan for protection of the northern spotted owl. Shortly after release of the ISC Strategy (Thomas Report) in 1990, Region 6 personnel made estimates of the sustainable harvest level under that strategy for Region 6 National Forests within range of the owl. Then they updated this estimate in 1992 for the Supplemental Environmental Impact Statement (EIS) for the Northern Spotted Owl. As part of the FEMAT effort, we ask Forest Service personnel to estimate the sustainable harvest level associated with the recovery plan for the owl (option 7). After correcting for differences in the area included, this most recent estimate (option 7) is 35 percent below the original estimate made for the ISC strategy in 1990 and 25 percent below the estimate made in the owl EIS in 1992 (Figure 1).

Thus the Forest Service's estimate of the harvest level on R-6 National Forests compatible with a high level of protection of the northern spotted owl has declined 35 percent over 3 years. Reasons for this decline include more realistic assessment of the 50-11-40 rule for matrix management that came with the Thomas Report, experience with implementing standards and guidelines from the National Forest Plans on the reduced land base available for timber production under the owl protection strategy, additional withdrawals (over those in the Thomas Report) associated with the recovery plan, and the change from estimating an allowable sale quantity to estimating a probable sale quantity.

Given this reduced estimate, assessment of the timber harvest cost of protecting habitat for other late successional species and threatened fish stocks starts from a much lower reference harvest level than would have been assumed in the past. While this result may be disheartening to policy-makers, I not sure how it could have been prevented. I have been part of the effort to estimate sustainable harvest levels in Region 6 for the last 10 years. In each case, we made our best effort to estimate the quantity in question given the forest management rules as we understood them at the time. Perhaps one mistake we made was to estimate upper limit (ceiling) harvest levels rather than probable harvest levels as it may have allowed the Forest Service to delay (until project planning) the development of harvest levels consistent with all its other objectives. If we had it to do over, I would have argued for a move to the "probable sale quantity" concept at a much earlier date.

4) In the FEMAT Report, we estimated a probable sale quantity for Forest Service and BLM lands within the owl region of 1.67 billion board feet/yr for the forest plans + the spotted owl recovery plan (option 7) and 1.08 billion for the Administration's proposed plan (option 9) (Table II-5 and Figure II-16 from the FEMAT Report (attached and labeled Table 1 and Figure 2)). Region 6 portions of these two estimates are 1.01 billion board feet (option 7) and .67 billion (option 9). The difference between the option 7 and option 9 estimates can be ascribed largely to protection of habitat for other late successional species (especially the marbled murrelet) and to protection of watersheds and riparian systems (especially habitat for potentially threatened fish stocks). In Table 1, we note that the probable sale levels given there should be within 10 percent of final results. We are currently finishing a detailed report on our procedures and results. I expect that our estimate of the probable sale quantity for option 9 will be between 1.0 and 1.1 billion in our final assessment, ie., within the predicted 10 percent of the 1.08 estimate in the FEMAT Report.

5) Adding 10% to the probable sale quantity for "other wood" often harvested along with the sound sawtimber of the probable sale quantity gives a average timber sales level for option 9 for the first decade of 1.1-1.2 billion board feet/yr. This projected level is approximately 25 percent of 1980-89 harvest from federal land in the owl region (a 75% reduction) and 48 percent of the 1990-1992 harvest from these forests (a 52 percent reduction) (Table 1). Other options give higher or lower harvest levels.

6) As pointed out in the FEMAT Report, some of the management rules and procedures for the different options make it difficult to determine fully the actual sale level that will result. I will concentrate on option 9, but most of the discussion here also applies to the other options:

a) Approximately 15 percent of the sale level in option 9 comes from Tier 1 key watersheds (those with potentially threatened fish stocks). Our estimate of the probable sale contribution of these areas is based on an interim set of rules for their management, but a "watershed assessment" will be needed before sales can go forward. We do not know when this assessment will be finished nor what its outcome will be. In the meantime, other parts of the forest could be the source of the Tier 1 key watershed's share of the harvest. Without some thought, these key watersheds may function somewhat like the roadless areas of the 80s: in the timber base but unavailable, with a resulting overemphasis on timber harvest from other lands. To avoid this problem, I urge that the Forest Service consider keeping the probable sale contribution for these watersheds separate (noninterchangeable) from the rest of the probable sale level such that the portion of the probable sale level ascribed to these areas actually must come from them.

b) With a few exceptions, we generally modeled the adaptive management areas of option 9 as contributing approximately the same harvest/suitable timber acre as if they were part of the matrix with no special additional prescriptions. This approach is consistent with the overall strategy that adaptive management areas should demonstrate innovative approaches to implement option 9 as opposed to having separate objectives of their own. Still, we do not know how much harvest will flow from the areas once their adaptive management approach is in place. As with Tier 1 key watersheds, I urge that the Forest Service consider keeping the probable sale contribution for these areas separate (noninterchangeable) from the rest of the probable sale level such that the portion of the probable sale level ascribed to these areas actually must come from them.

c) Like many of the options, option 9 calls for designation of "activity centers" for marbled murrelets and other species, as they are found, within which timber harvest will be prohibited or restricted. We allowed for the impact of only those sites that were found at the time of the analysis. I expect many more sites will be found, especially for the murrelet with a resulting impact on timber harvest levels.

d) It was difficult for us to capture fully the impact of the extensive riparian network in option 9 on the area available for timber production. Much of the timber production area will be in fairly small pieces and slivers between the riparian corridors---at least until watershed analysis is completed. While we did conduct an operability assessment, and a reduction for inoperable acres was factored into the probable sale quantity, I remain concerned that we have recognized the full extent of this problem.

e) Over time we would expect the sustainable harvest level to rise as the effect of intensive management in the matrix takes hold and a better balance of age classes occurs. In option 9, the sustainable harvest level for the first decade for Region 6 National Forests, as an example, assumes about 60 cubic feet/year from the suitable timber land while these sites should be capable of growth rates approaching at least 100 cubic feet/year. We would expect green tree retention and other objectives to reduce potential growth somewhat, but I still feel that the sustainable level over time may increase.

7) Numerous other issues exist over management of federal forests in the owl region under option 9 that could affect timber harvest levels there:

a) A number of mitigation steps are outlined in the FEMAT Report to increase the level of protection given to the habitat for different species if that is desired. Increasing habitat protection to an 80 percent likelihood of achieving stable, well-distributed populations, as an example, for species that do not attain that level of protection under option 9 (such as anadromous fish stocks) could have a significant impact on the probable sale quantity.

b) Theories about how to achieve sustainable forest ecosystems are rapidly evolving. Much of the thinking centers around an objective of reflecting historic (pre-European) patterns of forest structure and disturbance as the surest guide to sustainable forests, and I would expect forest plan revision to consider this guide. FEMAT did not directly address this issue in terms of matrix management. Rather FEMAT, in many alternatives such as option 9, utilized the matrix management approach of the forest plans slightly augmented by green tree retention requirements. Altering rotation length and other practices in the matrix to enable federal forests to reflect historic patterns of forest structure and disturbance could significantly affect timber harvest levels.

c) Many National Forests in Region 6 have already begun implementation of the Chief's new ecosystem policy. Green tree retention under this policy is often higher than the 15% called for under option 9. Therefore, implementation of option 9 could require a roll-back of these practices on some forests---always a hard thing to achieve---or the probable sale levels estimated here could prove inaccurate.

d) Most of the harvest in option 9 (and many other options) over the next decade will come from late-successional forest (over 80 years of age). Close to 50 percent will come from forest over 200 years of age. Thus late successional forest will remain the bulwark of the harvest in the next decade under option 9. On the four Cascade National Forests that will provide much of the Forest Service contribution to harvest under option 9 (Gifford Pinchot, Mt. Hood, Willamette, Umpqua), little other approach is possible given the age class distribution of the inventory (Figures 3 and 4) . While option 9 may reserve the lion's share of late successional forest on federal land, it does not escape the historic dependence on late-successional forest and old growth as the source of harvest volume. How publicly acceptable this policy will be remains to be seen.

8) We have analyzed the potential volume from thinning and catastrophic salvage in late successional reserves separate from the probable sale levels discussed above. Our findings to this point are:

a) Little volume could be produced from thinning managed stands in reserves in the first decade---the stands are just too young (generally less than 30 years of age) to contribute much volume except in a few places like the Oregon Coast. Next decade, though,

5

such harvest could began to contribute more volume. On the other hand, up to 50 million board feet/yr might be produced by allowing the thinning of <u>natural stands up to 80 years old</u> (the limit in option 9) if it can be shown that such action is neutral or beneficial to attainment of late successional habitat.

b) Harvesting much volume from catastrophic salvage under the rules of option 9 will be difficult given its requirements to leave enough dead trees to achieve natural levels of snags and coarse woody debris once late successional characteristics again occur (80-100 years). Most likely, salvage of only relatively small trees (under 20" diameter breast high) from large, heavily-impacted areas will be permitted. With most of the volume in the mature forests of the owl region occurring in trees over 20 inches in diameter, only limited salvage will be permitted after many fires. Even that activity may face many safety issues. Achieving even 50 million board feet/year of catastrophic salvage from reserves under historic disturbance rates would seem difficult.

9) Timber sales in the short-run that conform to option 9 will be difficult to develop from the enjoined sales given all the new reserve boundaries and management rules in the option. An initial estimate (Table 2, Figure 5) suggests that about 1/4-1/3 of the enjoined sale volume on the National Forests of Regions 5 and 6 might be available outside of controversial areas. That amount could increase or shrink further depending on how (and how fast) the option is implemented.

(Attachments follow:)

Figure 1.

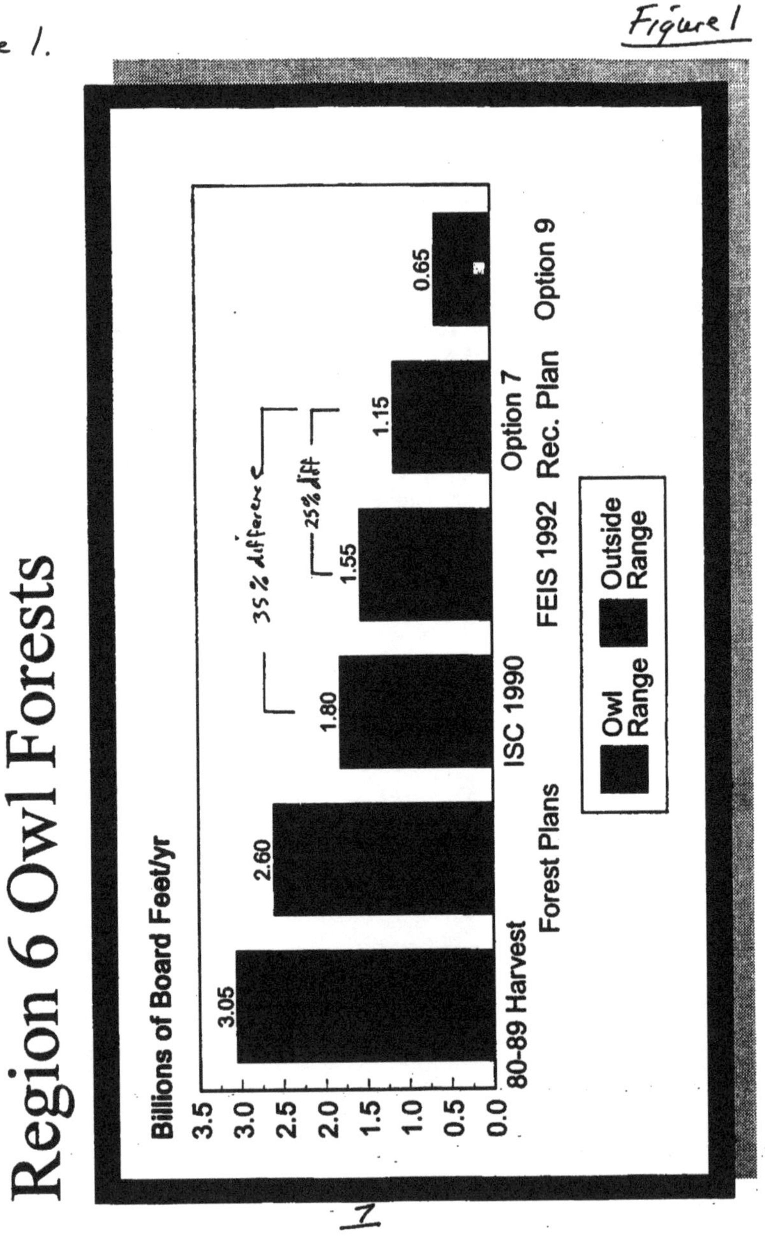
Figure 1
Region 6 Owl Forests
Billions of Board Feet/yr
3.5
3.0
2.5
2.0
1.5
1.0
0.5
0.0
3.05
2.60
1.80
1.55
1.15
0.65
80-89 Harvest
Forest Plans
ISC 1990
FEIS 1992
Option 7
Rec. Plan
Option 9
35% difference
25% diff
Owl Range
Outside Range
1

## Table 1

Table II-5. Historic federal harvests and probable annual average timber sales in the first decade by option.[a]

| Administrative Unit | Average Harvest | | Option[c] | | | | | | | | | |
|---|---|---|---|---|---|---|---|---|---|---|---|---|
| | 1980-89 | 1990-92 | 1 | 2 | 3 | 4 | 5 | 6 | 7 | 8 | 9 | 10 |
| National Forests- Owl Forests | | | million board feet, scribner | | | | | | | | | |
| **Region 6 - Owl Forests** | | | | | | | | | | | | |
| Western Washington | 824 | 404 | 22 | 69 | 75 | 67 | 119 | 87 | 186 | 133 | 131 | 94 |
| Eastern Washington | 195 | 124 | 11 | 31 | 33 | 30 | 26 | 37 | 47 | 65 | 47 | 52 |
| Western Oregon | 1902 | 897 | 68 | 207 | 239 | 284 | 392 | 300 | 716 | 473 | 429 | 357 |
| Eastern Oregon | 127 | 100 | 15 | 45 | 45 | 37 | 49 | 47 | 65 | 53 | 59 | 52 |
| Total | 3048 | 1525 | 116 | 352 | 391 | 418 | 585 | 471 | 1015 | 723 | 666 | 555 |
| **Region 5 - Owl Forests** | | | | | | | | | | | | |
| Total | 561 | 291 | 20 | 127 | 132 | 106 | 146 | 141 | 242 | 246 | 152 | 220 |
| **Bureau of Land Management - Owl Forests** | | | | | | | | | | | | |
| Western Oregon/Calif. | 880 | 568 | 41 | 134 | 142 | 146 | 177 | 158 | 406 | 298 | 260 | 200 |
| Eastern Oregon | 35 | 5 | 0 | 3 | 3 | 3 | 6 | 4 | 7 | 6 | 6 | 4 |
| Total | 915 | 573 | 41 | 137 | 145 | 149 | 183 | 162 | 413 | 304 | 266 | 204 |
| Total Owl Forests | 4524 | 2389 | 177 | 616 | 668 | 673 | 915 | 774 | 1669 | 1274 | 1084 | 979 |
| National Forests- NonOwl Forests[b] | | | | | | | | | | | | |
| **Region 6 - NonOwl Forests** | | | | | | | | | | | | |
| Eastern Washington | 134 | 138 | 102 | 102 | 102 | 102 | 102 | 102 | 102 | 102 | 102 | 102 |
| Eastern Oregon | 942 | 831 | 422 | 422 | 422 | 422 | 422 | 422 | 422 | 422 | 422 | 422 |
| Total NonOwl Forests | 1076 | 969 | 524 | 524 | 524 | 524 | 524 | 524 | 524 | 524 | 524 | 524 |

[a] Probable sale levels should be within 10 percent of the final number and include an "other wood" estimates. Ultimate numbers are "gross" volumes and thus exclude historic levels of other wood. Historic numbers for 1990-92 are estimates.

[b] Nonowl forests have not been subjected to rigorous analysis for the various alternatives and appear only for regional prior projections. Fate of the outside forests is highly uncertain in the present case.

[c] Volumes for Options 1, 3, and 10 are approximated on the basis of analysis on the other seven options.

128

Figure 2

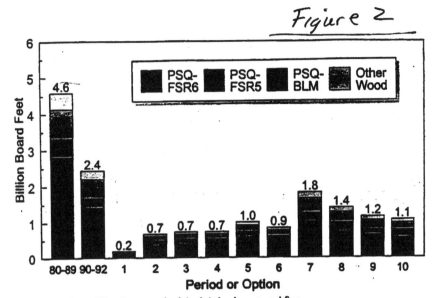

Figure II-16. Historic average for federal timber harvests and first decade's probable sale levels from federal forests within the impact region by agency ownership and option.

Figure 3.

Figure 3

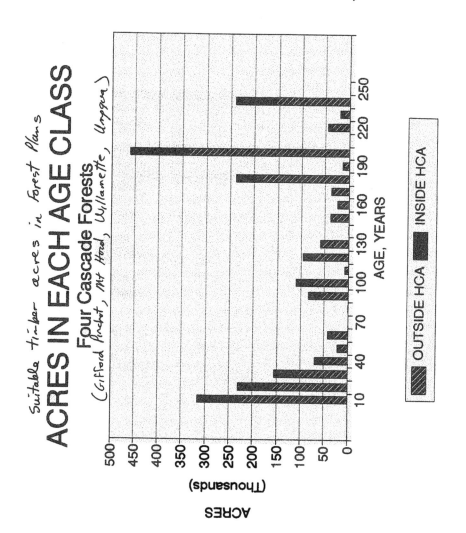

Suitable timber acres in forest plans

# ACRES IN EACH AGE CLASS
## Four Cascade Forests
(Gifford Pinchot, Mt Hood, Willamette, Umpqua)

Figure 4.

Figure 4

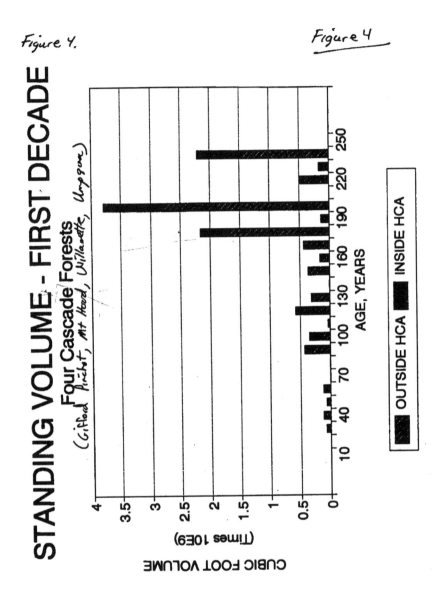

STANDING VOLUME - FIRST DECADE
Four Cascade Forests
(Gifford Pinchot, Mt Hood, Willamette, Umpqua)

CUBIC FOOT VOLUME
(Times 10E9)

AGE, YEARS

OUTSIDE HCA    INSIDE HCA

*Table 2*

Table VI-3. Sale estimates by sale category and Option 9 allocations for National Forests within the owl region.

| Land Allocation Classes | Category 1 (Sold & Awarded) | | Category 2 (Enjoined) | | Category 3 & 4[c] (Not Enjoined) | | Category 5 (Sold & Not Awarded) | |
|---|---|---|---|---|---|---|---|---|
| | Total Vol | Net of RR[a] | Total Vol | Net of RR[a] | Total Vol | Net of RR[a] | Total Vol | Net of RR[a] |
| | Millions of Board Feet | | | | | | | |
| Total Sales[b] | 1808.1 | 1413.8 | 1199.2 | 874.7 | 475.7 | 414.2 | 85.1 | 58.9 |
| I. Inside Murrelet Near Zone | 411.6 | 244.2 | 361.8 | 205.3 | 63.3 | 49.3 | 13.8 | 4.8 |
| A. Inside Reserves | 209.4 | 109.3 | 198.8 | 102.4 | 13.8 | 9.8 | 13.8 | 4.8 |
| 1. Inside Tier 1 Watersheds | 133.6 | 59.2 | 63.0 | 32.0 | 9.3 | 6.5 | 9.5 | 2.8 |
| 2. Outside Tier 1 Watersheds | 75.8 | 50.1 | 135.8 | 70.4 | 4.5 | 3.3 | 4.3 | 2.0 |
| B. Outside Reserves | 202.2 | 134.9 | 163.0 | 102.9 | 49.5 | 39.5 | 0 | 0 |
| 1. Inside Tier 1 Watersheds | 66.0 | 47.3 | 48.6 | 38.1 | 25.7 | 21.6 | 0 | 0 |
| 2. Outside Tier 1 Watersheds | 136.2 | 87.6 | 114.4 | 64.8 | 23.8 | 17.9 | 0 | 0 |
| II. Outside Murrelet Near Zone | 1396.5 | 1169.6 | 837.4 | 669.4 | 412.4 | 364.9 | 71.3 | 54.1 |
| A. Inside Reserves | 453.5 | 372.3 | 214.5 | 161.9 | 77.7 | 65.0 | 42.3 | 30.8 |
| 1. Inside Tier 1 Watersheds | 190.3 | 150.2 | 93.0 | 67.0 | 24.4 | 16.6 | 21.3 | 13.7 |
| 2. Outside Tier 1 Watersheds | 263.2 | 222.1 | 121.5 | 94.9 | 53.3 | 48.4 | 21.0 | 17.1 |
| B. Outside Reserves | 943.0 | 797.3 | 622.9 | 507.5 | 334.7 | 299.9 | 29.0 | 23.3 |
| 1. Inside Tier 1 Watersheds | 152.8 | 119.4 | 109.2 | 84.1 | 45.1 | 37.5 | 0 | 0 |
| 2. Outside Tier 1 Watersheds[d] | 790.2 | 667.9 | 513.7 | 423.4 | 289.6 | 262.4 | 29.0 | 23.3 |

[a] Time needed to do sale redesign to exclude RR (Riparian Reserve) volume is not known at this time.
[b] This does not exclude three other possible encumbrances: Colonel Nelson for the numbers quoted owl, Roadless Area designations, and tier 1 watersheds.
[c] Category 4 sales are not mapped. Assumed their total volume 66.3 million board feet is available outside of all Option 9 allocations.

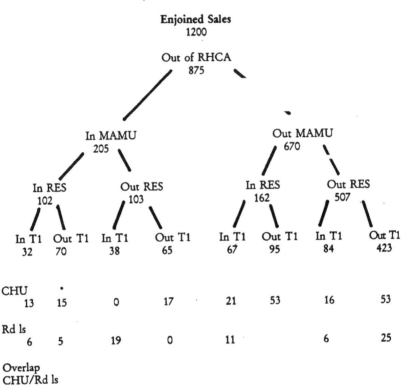

Region 5 and 6 Timber Sales and Sold Volume
Considered in the light of option 9

*Figure 5*

(Millions of board feet)

RHCA = Riparian habitat conservation area
In MAMU = In the near range of the marbled murrelet
In RES = In the reserves of option 9
In T1 = In tier 1 watersheds (those with potentially threatened fish stocks)
CHU = critical habitat units for the northern spotted owl
Rd ls = RARE II roadless areas
Overlap CHU/Rd ls = overlap of critical habitat and roadless areas

August 3, 1993

Mr. Victor M. Sher
Mr. Todd D. True
Sierra Club Legal Defense Fund
203 Hoge Building, Suite 705
Seattle, Washington 98104

Dear Mr. Sher and Mr. True:

Thank you for your letter offering to work with the Administration in a process to identify timber sale volume for release from the existing injunction in Seattle Audubon Society v. Lyons as soon as possible.

We welcome your offer. We also want to offer our commitment to pursuing this process for freeing sale volume pending the promulgation of a final plan at the end of this year. We believe that attempts to legislate "sufficiency" language that would seek to insulate the President's plan from the requirements of existing law or judicial review would undermine this process, and if this process is successful, we will continue to oppose any "sufficiency" legislation pending final promulgation of the President's plan.

We look forward to working with you in the next several weeks as we move forward with a scientifically sound, ecologically credible, and legally responsible program for the Federal forestlands of the Pacific Northwest.

Sincerely,

Bruce Babbitt
Secretary of the Interior

Mike Espy
Secretary of Agriculture

93-664 ENR
July 16, 1993

# CRS Report for Congress

Congressional Research Service • The Library of Congress

## The Clinton Administration's Forest Plan
## for the Pacific Northwest

Ross W. Gorte
Specialist in Natural Resources Policy
Environment and Natural Resources Policy Division

## INTRODUCTION

On April 2, 1993, President Clinton fulfilled a campaign promise by convening a forest conference in Portland, OR, to address the gridlock over management of the Federal forestlands in the Pacific Northwest and the resulting effects on communities and the regional economy. Many interests and ideas were heard by the President, Vice President Gore, numerous Cabinet Members, and other Presidential advisors. At the close of the conference, the President committed to preparing a plan within 60 days to address the problems.

Intensive efforts following the forest conference led to development of a background paper with 10 options. This paper has not been distributed, because elements of it are still being discussed and modified, but briefings and press reports have disclosed many of the pieces. "Option 9" of the background paper appears to be the basis for the proposal released by the White House on July 1, 1993: *The Forest Plan for a Sustainable Economy and a Sustainable Environment*. This plan is composed of three major pieces: forest management, economic development, and agency coordination.

## FOREST MANAGEMENT

The forest management segment of the plan was based on a presumption that current legal requirements for Federal land management would not be altered. The plan is described as using watersheds as the fundamental building blocks for planning and decisionmaking. It proposes reserve areas, adaptive management areas, and a total harvest level for the Forest Service and Bureau of Land Management (BLM). While congressional insulation of the plan from judicial review was discussed, such protection was not proposed in the plan.

To resolve the legal challenges and lift the existing injunctions against the Forest Service and BLM, the forest management segment of the plan must be approved by the courts as fulfilling the land management laws: the National Forest Management Act (NFMA), the Federal Land Policy and Management Act (FLPMA), the National Environmental Policy Act (NEPA), *et al.*. The plan will

135

CRS-2

be part of a draft Supplemental Environmental Impact Statement, which will be
submitted to Judge Dwyer of the Federal District Court for Western Washington
for the injunction against the Forest Service. It is unclear, at this time, whether
the court will find that the plan meets the legal requirements, and how the plan
and Judge Dwyer's decision might affect other lawsuits and the recovery plan
for the spotted owl.

## Reserve Areas

The plan proposes reserve areas based on watersheds, old growth forests,
and "designated conservation areas to protect specific species." While State-level
maps of the reserve areas exist, the plan does not specify the acreage reserved
or the distribution of that acreage by Federal unit (national forest, etc.).

The plan proposes "very limited activities" in the reserves, but allows timber
salvage and thinning "where the primary objective ... is to accelerate the development of old growth conditions." Environmental groups have expressed concern
about the potential misuse of salvage and thinning – to produce timber for
industrial production, with little regard to ecosystem health. This concern is
bolstered by a report from the Office of Technology Assessment noting that the
Forest Service financial and managerial control systems focus on timber output
and that the agency does not have adequate measures of ecosystem health.[1]
Thus, while such operations might promote old growth conditions, concern over
their level and control to achieve the stated purposes may be warranted.

## Adaptive Management Areas

The plan proposes 10 adaptive management areas of 78,000 to 380,000
acres each. As with the reserve areas, State-level maps show the adaptive
management areas, but the plan itself does not identify the total acreage or the
distribution of the adaptive management areas by Federal unit.

The adaptive management areas are intended to provide "intensive ecological experimentation and social innovation to develop and demonstrate new
ways to integrate ecological and economic objectives and allow for local
involvement in defining the future." A "rigorous monitoring and research
program" is proposed to assess the results and effectiveness of the efforts.

Implementation is the key to whether this approach is successful. The
Forest Service and BLM are both currently required to include public participation in their planning and management decisions, but local and national disagreements on management direction still exist. Furthermore, Forest Service
monitoring of forest plan implementation, required by NFMA, has been weak,
at best.[2] Thus, the agencies' abilities to achieve the stated goals are uncertain.

---

[1]U.S. Congress, Office of Technology Assessment. *Forest Service Planning:
Accommodating Uses, Producing Outputs, and Sustaining Ecosystems.* OTA-F-505.
Washington, DC: U.S. Govt. Print. Off., Feb. 1992.

[2]*Ibid.*

## Harvest Levels

The plan proposes "a sustainable timber harvest of 1.2 billion board feet annually on the spotted owl forests." Presumably, this includes not only the national forests west of the Cascade crest, but also the BLM lands in western Oregon, and national forests in northern California and east of the Cascade crest that contain spotted owl habitat. This harvest level apparently excludes harvests from some of the national forests in Washington and Oregon and most of the national forests in California. The distribution of this harvest by agency and Federal unit, however, is not specified.

This sale level is substantially below sales and harvests from the affected Federal lands over the past 30 years. However, some decline from peak harvest levels of the late 1980s is clearly not due to spotted owl protection.[3] Sale levels in the current forest plans have also been criticized as being unsustainable. Nonetheless, the proposed sale program is only about half the level that was projected under the recommendations of the Interagency Scientific Committee (the ISC or Thomas Report).[4] On the other hand, it is nearly double the sale program that has been achieved under the current injunctions. It is unclear, and not documented in the proposed plan, whether this decline either is larger than necessary or is even sufficient to meet the legal obligations of the agencies.

Regardless of whether the courts view the plan as adequate to lift the injunctions, generally imposed because of apparent violations of the land management laws, proposals for Federal actions (including timber salvage sales and thinning) must still be submitted for consultation with the Fish and Wildlife Service or the National Marine Fisheries Service under the Endangered Species Act (ESA).[5] In general, Federal actions cannot jeopardize threatened or endangered species or adversely modify their critical habitat. Thus, the forest plan must be submitted for consultation under ESA; or more likely, agency actions taken under the plan will probably be submitted for consultation, since the consequences of the plan may be insufficiently detailed to assess jeopardy or adverse habitat modification. Because the plan differs markedly from previous owl conservation plans (e.g., the ISC Report and the draft recovery plan), and because it might affect spotted owls, marbled murrelets, and listed salmon populations, consultations on the plan or on actions under the plan could be time consuming.

The plan proposes four additional steps to ease the impact of the reduced timber supplies from Federal lands. One is an unspecified new rule from the

[3]See: U.S. Library of Congress, Congressional Research Service. *Economic Impacts of Protecting Spotted Owls: A Comparison and Analysis of Existing Studies.* [by Ross W. Gorte.] CRS Report for Congress 92-922 ENR. Washington, DC: Dec. 7, 1992.

[4]*Ibid.*

[5]For more on this situation in the Northwest, see: U.S. Library of Congress, Congressional Research Service. *Spotted Owls and Northwest Forests.* CRS Issue Brief IB93015. Washington, DC: updated periodically.

Fish and Wildlife Service to ease timber harvesting restrictions on non-federal lands inhabited by spotted owls; however, this may be inconsistent with the ESA, at least until a recovery plan has been completed. The second is Federal assistance for backlogged timber sales on Indian reservations, but where, why, and how many sales are backlogged is unclear. The third step is to restrict the use of certain tax expenditures, to curtail tax assistance for log exports.

The fourth step is to accelerate the sale of dead and dying timber in eastern Washington and Oregon. Many eastside forest ecosystems have allegedly been damaged by past management practices and prolonged drought, and accelerating the salvage program is proposed as a way both to improve the health of these ecosystems and to provide timber. However, the traditional focus on timber outputs, the inadequate measures of forest health, and the results of past mismanagement raise concerns about the effectiveness of the proposal, and whether it would be conducted within the current national forest planning process.

## ECONOMIC DEVELOPMENT

The Northwest Economic Adjustment Initiative is the segment of the President's forest plan aimed at assisting the economic transition in the Pacific Northwest. The controversy between industry and environmental groups over the past several years has centered on forest management issues, with less attention to the subsequent and related economic adjustment. Nonetheless, the debate over the economic transition has raised concerns about the level of funding needed, the distribution of assistance, and the effectiveness of the delivery system.

The Northwest Economic Adjustment Initiative targets four groups for assistance: workers and families; communities and infrastructure; business and industry; and ecosystem investment. In addition, the plan proposes a Northwest Economic Adjustment Fund, with discretion for the States on how best to use the funds. Proposed funding for the Northwest Economic Adjustment Initiative is $1.2 billion over 5 years, including $270 million for FY1994. The FY1994 funding is probably based on the President's budget request; the amount needed to achieve the desired levels may be higher (or lower) than these estimates, depending on the changes made in the agencies' budgets by Congress. Some of the funding may be additional appropriations, but some will be redirected from other program and other regions.

Finally, the plan supports terminating the authority to use certain general export tax expenditures for the export of unprocessed timber, as noted above; the Senate included a provision to enact this change in the tax laws in H.R. 2264, the Omnibus Budget Reconciliation Act of 1993, but a conference must still resolve this and other differences between the House and Senate versions of the bill. It is unclear whether any of the budget savings from this change in the tax laws has been included in the proposed $1.2 billion for the Northwest Economic Adjustment Initiative.

138

CRS-5

**Workers and Families**

The plan proposes an increase in funding under title III of the Job Training Partnership Act (JTPA) for assisting job searches and retraining and relocating workers; this assistance is available for all displaced workers, not just those in the timber industry. For FY1994, a 110-percent ($22 million) increase in funds is proposed for the Northwest.

**Communities and Infrastructure**

The plan proposes stable payments to the counties, in lieu of property taxes for the tax-exempt Federal lands, to replace the timber receipt-sharing system that has provided widely fluctuating annual payments. Additional funding for the Northwest is proposed through the Rural Development Administration, Community Development Block Grants, and other programs; for FY1994, the increase is to be 25 percent ($75 million) over the original budget request for these programs. These funds are intended to assist communities in planning for economic development and diversification and in providing the necessary infrastructure for such development.

**Business and Industry**

The plan proposes a 47-percent ($77 million) increase in funding for the Northwest through the Rural Development Administration, the Small Business Administration, and other business assistance programs for FY1994. The funds in these programs are intended to improve access to capital, to expand technical assistance, and to enhance access to domestic and global markets.

**Ecosystem Investment**

The plan proposes to increase funds for watershed maintenance, ecosystem restoration and research, environmental monitoring, and forest stewardship. Most of these efforts will be aimed at Federal lands, but forest stewardship will include assistance for private, nonindustrial forestlands. For FY1994, the proposed increase is 19 percent ($82 million), funded through the Forest Service, BLM, Fish and Wildlife Service, and Environmental Protection Agency.

**AGENCY COORDINATION**

Improving agency coordination is the third major segment of President Clinton's forest plan. The plan states that this segment is essential, because the various agencies have been seen as acting "in isolation or even at cross purposes in managing federal forest lands."

The plan proposes "forest planning based on watersheds and "physiographic provinces"" with analyses by "provincial-level teams" that include the relevant Federal and State agencies and tribes and that would involve "all affected parties in the discussions." The benefits of watershed-level planning have been long debated in land management literature. However, it is unclear how this new planning will mesh with the existing land and resource management planning

CRS-6

procedures for units of the National Forest System under NFMA and for BLM lands under FLPMA. The current procedures are embodied in regulations that are binding on the two agencies.

The plan also proposes "a new inter-agency Geographic Information System [GIS] data base." GIS systems are indeed useful in coordinating data collection and analysis, and this will likely improve interagency coordination. Furthermore, GIS technology has advanced rapidly in the past few years. However, the hardware and software needed to use GIS systems are expensive, and the plan provides no information on how the initial investment and annual maintenance of the database will be funded.

Finally, the plan proposes revising the consultation process under ESA to include the relevant agency – the Fish and Wildlife Service and/or the National Marine Fisheries Service – early in the planning processes of the other agencies, and possibly at a scale larger than individual projects. Early involvement can certainly help avoid many of the problems and apparent contradictions in the existing process. However, early involvement is already feasible and available, and it is unclear what specific changes in ESA or its implementing regulations might be offered. It is also unclear how "the use, where appropriate, of regional consultations" would mesh with existing planning and decisionmaking processes of the Forest Service and BLM.

## CONCLUSIONS

President Clinton's forest plan is an attempt to resolve the continuing controversy over forest management in the Pacific Northwest. Because of the longstanding polarization of interests, it is virtually impossible to craft a plan that would be widely accepted. The proposed harvest level is a very substantial drop from record levels of the late 1980s, but whether the decline is sufficient or is more than necessary to meet the requirements of environmental laws and regulations is unclear. Moreover, the plan might be sufficient to lift the current injunctions, but the plan or the subsequent activities must still be submitted to the Fish and Wildlife Service and/or the National Marine Fisheries Service for consultation under ESA.

The reserve areas and adaptive management areas, though not yet clearly identified, appear to be based on reasonable scientific principles of forest management. However, their proper implementation is essential, and many critics do not trust the agencies to implement the plan to achieve the specified goals. Substantial funding over 5 years is proposed for workers, communities, businesses, and ecosystem investment, but whether the funding levels and delivery mechanisms are adequate and attainable is unknown. The efforts to improve coordination among agencies are desirable, but previous efforts at interagency coordination have often proven ineffective.